How to Use This Book

Look for these special features in this book:

SIDEBARS, **CHARTS**, **GRAPHS**, and original **MAPS** expand your understanding of what's being discussed—and also make useful sources for classroom reports.

FAQs answer common **F**requently **A**sked **Q**uestions about people, places, and things.

WOW FACTORS offer "Who knew?" facts to keep you thinking.

TRAVEL GUIDE gives you tips on exploring the state—either in person or right from your chair!

PROJECT ROOM provides fun ideas for school assignments and incredible research projects. Plus, there's a guide to primary sources—what they are and how to cite them.

Please note: All statistics are as up-to-date as possible at the time of publication. Population data is taken from the 2010 census.

Consultants: William Loren Katz; Brent Riffel, *Arkansas Historical Quarterly*; John Van Brahana, Department of Geosciences, University of Arkansas; Jay H. Casey, Assistant Professor, University of Arkansas

Book production by The Design Lab

Library of Congress Cataloging-in-Publication Data
Prentzas, G. S.
 Arkansas / by G.S. Prentzas. — Revised edition.
 pages cm. — (America the beautiful, third series)
 Includes bibliographical references and index.
 Audience: Ages 9–12.
 ISBN 978-0-531-28276-2 (lib. bdg.)
 1. Arkansas—Juvenile literature. I. Title.
 F411.3.P74 2014
 976.7—dc23   2013044316

2 3 4 5 6 7 8 9 10 R 24 23 22 21 20 19 18 17 16 15

Revised Edition

AMERICA ★ THE ★ BEAUTIFUL

Arkansas

BY G. S. PRENTZAS

Third Series, Revised Edition

Children's Press®
An Imprint of Scholastic Inc.
New York ★ Toronto ★ London ★ Auckland ★ Sydney
Mexico City ★ New Delhi ★ Hong Kong
Danbury, Connecticut

CONTENTS

ARKANSAS

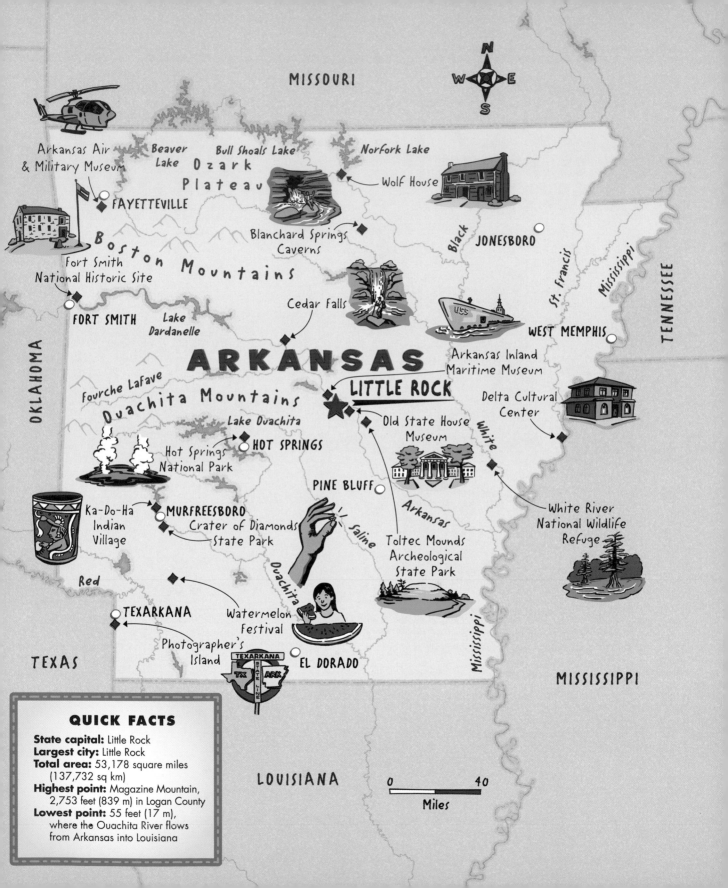

MISSOURI

N W E S

Arkansas Air & Military Museum

Beaver Lake

Bull Shoals Lake

Norfork Lake

Wolf House

Ozark Plateau

FAYETTEVILLE

Blanchard Springs Caverns

Black

JONESBORO

St. Francis

Mississippi

TENNESSEE

Fort Smith National Historic Site

Boston Mountains

FORT SMITH

Lake Dardanelle

Cedar Falls

WEST MEMPHIS

Arkansas Inland Maritime Museum

OKLAHOMA

ARKANSAS

LITTLE ROCK

Fourche Lafave

Ouachita Mountains

Old State House Museum

Delta Cultural Center

White

Lake Ouachita

HOT SPRINGS

Hot Springs National Park

PINE BLUFF

Arkansas

White River National Wildlife Refuge

Ka-Do-Ha Indian Village

MURFREESBORO
Crater of Diamonds State Park

Saline

Toltec Mounds Archeological State Park

Red

Ouachita

TEXARKANA

Watermelon Festival

Photographer's Island

TEXARKANA STATE LINE
TX ARK

EL DORADO

Mississippi

TEXAS

MISSISSIPPI

LOUISIANA

0   40
Miles

QUICK FACTS

State capital: Little Rock
Largest city: Little Rock
Total area: 53,178 square miles
(137,732 sq km)
Highest point: Magazine Mountain,
2,753 feet (839 m) in Logan County
Lowest point: 55 feet (17 m),
where the Ouachita River flows
from Arkansas into Louisiana

Welcome to Arkansas!

HOW DID ARKANSAS GET ITS NAME?

Arkansas's name comes from a Native American group that lived west of the Mississippi River and north of the Arkansas River (which is also named after them). They called themselves Quapaws, but Native Americans who lived in the northern part of the Mississippi River valley and spoke the Sioux language called them *Akansa*, a word that means "people of the south wind." French explorers Louis Joliet and Jacques Marquette labeled the Quapaw nation's territory "Akansea" on a map they made of the Mississippi River in 1673. This eventually became Arkansas.

ARKANSAS

8

READ ABOUT

A view of Petit
Jean State Park

CHAPTER ONE

LAND

★

RKANSAS IS CALLED THE NATURAL STATE. From its highest point on Magazine Mountain, at 2,753 feet (839 meters), to its lowest point at 55 feet (17 m) where the Ouachita River flows into Louisiana, the state boasts enchanting mountains, secluded river valleys, vast woodlands, and many scenic waterways. Arkansas encompasses 53,178 square miles (137,732 square kilometers), making it about the same size as New York or Alabama. A wide variety of plants and animals, from wildflowers to razorback hogs, live in these many different environments.

Arkansas Topography

Use the color-coded elevation chart to see on the map Arkansas's high points (orange) and low points (green to dark green). Elevation is measured as the distance above or below sea level.

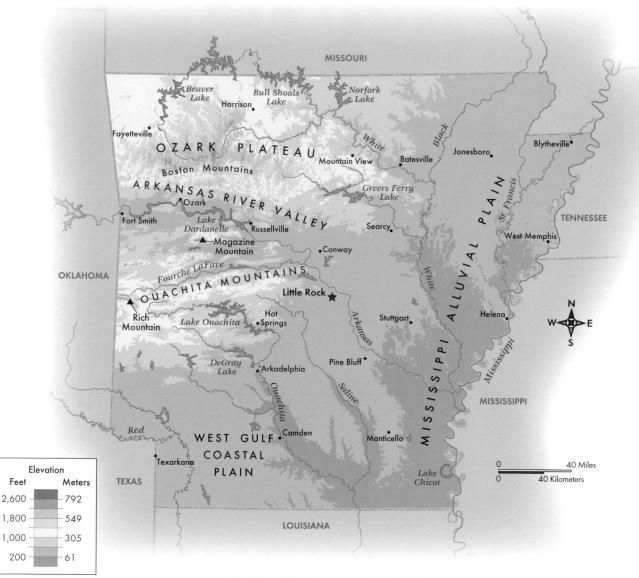

Elevation	
Feet	Meters
2,600	792
1,800	549
1,000	305
200	61

WATER AND ROCK

Would you believe that until about 37 million years ago, seawater covered nearly half of Arkansas? Look at a map. The present-day cities of Little Rock, Pine Bluff, and Jonesboro would have been underwater back then! Today, geologists find fossils of sea creatures, such as sharks and oysters, throughout the state.

An even more ancient ocean covered the southwest part of the state hundreds of millions of years ago. Sand and clay accumulated on the bottom of this sea, and thick layers of salt occurred around its margins. Around 300 million years ago, currents of melted rock deep within the earth pushed North America and South America into each other, causing the seafloor in what is now Arkansas to buckle upward. This collision formed the Ouachita Mountains. For millions of years, **erosion** has been wearing down the mountains, so today they are much smaller and less rugged than they once were.

Erosion of the mountains deposited sand and gravel along the rivers in the highlands. In the lowlands, layers of sand and clay are reminders that the area was a seafloor for millions of years. Windblown dust also piled up on top of the ground in the lowlands. For the past several thousand years, floods along the Mississippi River and other waterways have left sand and other **sediment** along Arkansas's riverbanks.

Arkansas Geo-Facts

Along with the state's geographical highlights, this chart ranks Arkansas's land, water, and total area compared to all other states.

Total area; rank . . . . . 53,178 square miles (137,732 sq km); 29th
Land; rank . . . . 52,030 square miles (134,758 sq km); 27th
Water; rank . . . . 1,149 square miles (2,976 sq km); 31st
Inland water; rank . . . 1,149 square miles (2,976 sq km); 19th
Geographic center . . . . . In Pulaski County, about 12 miles (19 km) northwest of Little Rock
Latitude . . . . .33° N to 36°30' N
Longitude . . . . 89°41' W to 94°42' W
Highest point . . . . Magazine Mountain, 2,753 feet (839 m) in Logan County
Lowest point . . . . 55 feet (17 m), where the Ouachita River flows from Arkansas into Louisiana
Largest city . . . . .Little Rock
Longest river . . . . .Mississippi

Source: U.S. Census Bureau, 2010 census

 Rhode Island, the smallest state, could fit inside Arkansas 34 times.

WORDS TO KNOW

erosion *the gradual wearing away of rock or soil by physical breakdown, chemical solution, or water*

sediment *material eroded from rocks and deposited elsewhere by wind, water, or glaciers*

One of the many caves found in Ozark National Forest

Mammoth Spring produces more than 200 million gallons (757 million liters) of water on an average day! It is the largest spring in Arkansas.

LAND REGIONS

Arkansas has five main land regions. Three of them—the Ozark Plateau, the Arkansas River Valley, and the Ouachita Mountains—are highlands. These are located in the north and the west. The West Gulf Coastal Plain and Mississippi **Alluvial Plain** regions make up the lowlands, which are in the south and the east.

The Ozark Plateau

The mountainous area known as the Ozark Plateau extends across parts of Arkansas, Missouri, Oklahoma,

Kansas, and Illinois. It covers most of northwestern and north-central Arkansas. In Arkansas, the Ozarks have rolling hills, flat ridges, and deep river valleys. The region is filled with rivers, lakes, waterfalls, and mineral springs. The White River attracts trout fishers. The Buffalo National River in the Ozarks was the nation's first waterway to be placed under federal government protection. It's one of the few major American rivers that has no dams.

The Ozarks are best known for their valleys (known locally as hollows) and rounded hills (known locally as knobs). Throughout the Ozarks, rainwater has seeped underground and carved out caves in the region's soft limestone rock. Around 2,000 of these caves have been discovered, and several have more than 10 miles (16 km) of mapped passageways underground! In many of these caves, dripping water has left behind minerals that built up into **stalactites**, **stalagmites**, and other formations. Some of these formations look like draperies, others like pearls. Many people visit Blanchard Springs Caverns near the town of Mountain View to see the amazing formations.

The Arkansas River Valley

The Arkansas River Valley region separates the Ozark Plateau from the Ouachita Mountains to the south. The main feature of the region is the Arkansas River, which lies in a wide valley. Arkansas's tallest mountain, Magazine Mountain, reaches 2,753 feet (839 m) above sea level on the south side of the Arkansas River Valley.

In the days before roads were built, the Arkansas River was a major transportation route, so cities grew along the river. Today, most of Arkansas's large cities, including Little Rock and Fort Smith, lie in the Arkansas River Valley.

FAQ

Q8 WHAT IS A MINERAL SPRING?

A8 Springs are pools or streams of water that flow out of cracks in the ground or from cave entrances. A mineral water spring is one in which the water has dissolved soil and rocks while flowing underground so that the water contains more minerals than usual. The water from many mineral springs in Arkansas has been bottled and is sometimes sold as a health aid.

WORDS TO KNOW

alluvial plain *an area that is created when sand, soil, and rocks are carried by water and dropped in a certain place*

stalactites *columns or pillars formed on the ceiling of a cave from dripping groundwater*

stalagmites *columns or pillars formed on the floor of a cave from dripping groundwater*

Sunset over the Ouachita Mountains

More than 70,000 diamonds have been found in Crater of Diamonds State Park. In June 2007, a 13-year-old girl found a 2.9-carat diamond!

The Ouachita Mountains

The Ouachita Mountains lie south of the Arkansas River Valley, near the western side of the state. Most mountain ranges in the United States run north to south, but the ridges and ravines in the Ouachitas run east to west. Rich Mountain is the Ouachitas' tallest peak. At 2,681 feet (817 m), it is the second-highest point in the state.

The Ouachita Mountains are dotted with crystal-clear lakes, quartz mineral mines, and hot mineral springs (the water is warmed by the heat of the earth—the deeper you go, the hotter it gets). The only diamond mine in North America that is open to the public is located just south of the Ouachitas, near the town of Murfreesboro.

The West Gulf Coastal Plain

The West Gulf Coastal Plain spreads up from the Gulf of Mexico. It runs through eastern Texas, northwestern Louisiana, and into southwestern Arkansas and neighboring Oklahoma. The ancient ocean waters that once covered this land left behind sandy clay soil. Dense forests of pine trees, which grow well in sandy soil, now cover the region. The West Gulf Coastal Plain has many oil and natural gas deposits. The state's lowest point is located in the southern part of the West Gulf Coastal Plain, where the Ouachita River flows into Louisiana. The Red River also runs through this region.

The Mississippi Alluvial Plain

The Mississippi River forms the entire eastern border of Arkansas, and the Mississippi Alluvial Plain covers the eastern one-third of the state. This mostly flat area, also known as the Delta, is filled with swamps, prairies, and rich farmland. Today, the Mississippi Alluvial Plain is the state's primary agricultural region. Fields of rice, cotton, and soybeans extend for miles. In fact, Arkansas is the top rice-producing state in the country, and almost all of it comes from the Delta. Lake Chicot, the state's largest natural lake, is located in this region in southeastern Arkansas. It is the largest oxbow lake in North America.

The Mississippi Alluvial Plain has two unusual physical features. **Bayou** Bartholomew flows for 359 miles (578 km) from near Pine Bluff into northern Louisiana.

SEE IT HERE!

CRATER OF DIAMONDS STATE PARK

In 1906, diamonds were discovered in a large crater near Murfreesboro. Scientists think these diamonds were formed more than 3 billion years ago many miles underground. About 95 million years ago, a volcanic eruption brought the diamonds close to the earth's surface. Over the years, erosion exposed the diamonds. Today, Crater of Diamonds State Park is the only diamond-producing site in the world that is open to the public. The largest diamond discovered by a park visitor was a 16-carat diamond found in 1975.

FAQ

Q: WHAT IS AN OXBOW LAKE?

A: It's a lake that forms when a river carves a new course during a flood, taking a shorter route and cutting off a curve in the river. The separated curve is no longer part of the river. Instead, it becomes a U-shaped lake.

WORD TO KNOW

bayou *a stream that runs slowly through a swamp and leads to or from a river*

FRIEND OF THE BAYOU

A former school superintendent, Dr. Curtis Merrell founded an organization to preserve the natural beauty of Bayou Bartholomew. The stream had once been unspoiled, but by the early 1990s, it had become polluted, jammed with logs, and full of sediment. Since 1995, the Bayou Bartholomew Alliance, the organization Merrell started, has worked with many different state and federal government agencies to reclaim the bayou. Projects include testing the bayou's water quality, breaking up logjams, and strengthening the bayou's banks.

It is the longest bayou in the United States and is surrounded by swampy land. The region's other unusual feature is Crowley's Ridge, a narrow, densely forested strip of high ground. The ridge ranges in width from 0.5 mile to 12 miles (0.8 to 19 km) and stretches north to south for 200 miles (322 km). In some places, Crowley's Ridge rises 500 feet (152 m) above sea level, looming over the surrounding lowlands.

Sunrise at Bayou Bartholomew near Pine Bluff

CLIMATE

Arkansas has a mostly moderate climate, although the weather in the highlands and the lowlands differs greatly. In winter, the low elevation and the effect of the distant warm waters of the Gulf of Mexico keep the air temperatures mild in the lowlands. In the highlands, however, temperatures often plunge below freezing. Summers are hot and humid in the lowlands but cooler in the highlands. The state generally gets plenty of rain.

Tornadoes are common, particularly in the West Gulf Coastal Plain. In February 2008, a tornado swept across north-central Arkansas, killing 14 people and injuring many others. In 2011, Hot Springs and Vilonia fell victim to a wave of tornadoes that caused four deaths and serious damage to the towns.

Flooding is also common. After a devastating flood in 1927, state and federal agencies built dams, **levees**, and flood walls to lessen flood damage. In 2010, heavy rains caused flooding in the Albert Pike Recreational Area, resulting in the death of 20 people.

PLANT LIFE

From the knobs of the Ozarks to the swamps of the Delta, Arkansas has a diverse landscape with many different environments for plant life. More than half of the state is

THE GREAT FLOOD

The Great Mississippi River Flood of 1927 started in April. An unusually warm spring caused snow in Canada and the northern United States to thaw quickly. The snowmelt, combined with heavy spring rains in the South, caused the Mississippi River to swell. Many rivers throughout the Mississippi River valley overflowed their banks, and so much water surged down the Mississippi that its water level rose tens of feet higher than average. That wall of water rushed into Arkansas's White River, causing it to flow backward for several days!

WORD TO KNOW

levees *human-made wall-like embankments, often made of earth, built along a river to control flooding*

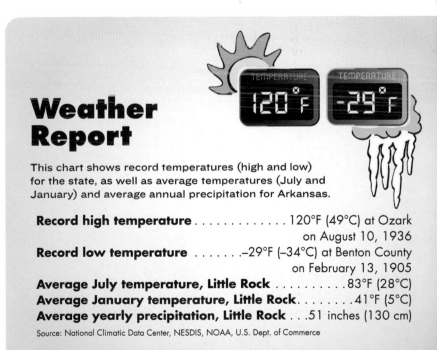

Weather Report

This chart shows record temperatures (high and low) for the state, as well as average temperatures (July and January) and average annual precipitation for Arkansas.

Record high temperature . . . . 120°F (49°C) at Ozark on August 10, 1936
Record low temperature . . . . –29°F (–34°C) at Benton County on February 13, 1905
Average July temperature, Little Rock . . . . 83°F (28°C)
Average January temperature, Little Rock . . . . 41°F (5°C)
Average yearly precipitation, Little Rock . . .51 inches (130 cm)

Source: National Climatic Data Center, NESDIS, NOAA, U.S. Dept. of Commerce

forested. Ash, hickory, maple, oak, and other hardwood trees are common in the highlands. Forests of loblolly pine and shortleaf pine cover the West Gulf Coastal Plain. Yellow poplars grow along Crowley's Ridge. Flowering trees, such as dogwood and azalea, are abundant throughout the state.

Many wildflowers, such as bluebells, water lilies, and yellow jasmine, grow throughout Arkansas. Wild orchids, called lady's slippers, grow in the West Gulf Coastal Plain's pine forests.

ANIMAL LIFE

Arkansas has numerous wilderness areas, which provide habitat for many types of mammals. Rabbits, raccoons, skunks, foxes, and deer make their homes in the state's forests and fields. Bobcats and bears live in the highlands. Bears were so common in the 1800s that Arkansas was known as the Bear State.

Blooming dogwood trees in an Arkansas forest

Red foxes like this one live in the Ozarks.

Arkansas's many streams, rivers, and lakes teem with fish. Bass and catfish are common throughout the state, while trout live in the cold, spring-fed rivers of the Ozarks. Crawfish, a small freshwater crustacean (bigger than a shrimp, smaller than a lobster), are plentiful in the Delta. Arkansas also has abundant butterflies. Magazine Mountain is home to dozens of butterfly species.

Nearly 400 types of birds live in or pass through Arkansas. The state is located on the Mississippi flyway, the route used by many songbirds and waterfowl to migrate from north to south and back again. Common birds include cardinals, mockingbirds, and robins.

ENVIRONMENTAL ISSUES

People have had a major impact on Arkansas's environment. Loggers have cut down pine trees through-

THE ARKANSAS RAZORBACK

The state's best-known animal is the Arkansas razorback. These hogs live in wooded areas throughout the state. They got their name from their prominent, hairy backbone. Males grow up to 5 feet (1.5 m) long and can weigh as much as 300 pounds (136 kilograms). Razorbacks can have sharp tusks, are very smart, and can run as fast as 35 miles per hour (56 kph). They can be dangerous if they feel threatened, and they cause many problems. They destroy plants while foraging for food and can transmit diseases to domestic animals. The University of Arkansas adopted the fierce razorback as the mascot for its sports teams.

ENDANGERED ANIMALS

The U.S. Fish and Wildlife Service has identified a number of plant and animal species in Arkansas as **endangered** or **threatened**. One of those species, the red-cockaded woodpecker, lives in the West Gulf Coastal Plain's pine forests. Another bird, the ivory-billed woodpecker, was thought to be extinct because none had been seen in many years, but a recent sighting in the bayous attracted worldwide attention. Scientists continue to debate whether any of these magnificent birds remain. Three kinds of endangered bats, including the Ozark big-eared bat, live in caves in Arkansas's highlands.

Red-cockaded woodpecker

Blackbirds gather at a winter roost near Brinkley.

WORDS TO KNOW

endangered *in danger of becoming extinct throughout all or part of a range*

threatened *likely to become endangered in the foreseeable future*

out the West Gulf Coastal Plain for wood and pine gum. Farmers have worn out soil by growing rice and cotton year after year. Today, the biggest threat to the state's environment is water pollution. Industry, especially chicken farms in the northwest, has polluted the state's waterways. Leaks from city sewage treatment plants and waste containers at hog farms add to the pollution.

In recent decades, state officials and citizens have worked together to repair the damage. In 1996, Arkansas voters agreed to tax themselves to provide funds for various state agencies that protect natural resources, including the Game and Fish Commission and the Keep Arkansas Beautiful Commission. Because the state's natural areas have created a large tourism industry, many Arkansans believe that it will benefit everyone if their state's natural heritage is preserved.

Arkansas National Park Areas

This map shows some of Arkansas's national parks, monuments, preserves, and other areas protected by the National Park Service.

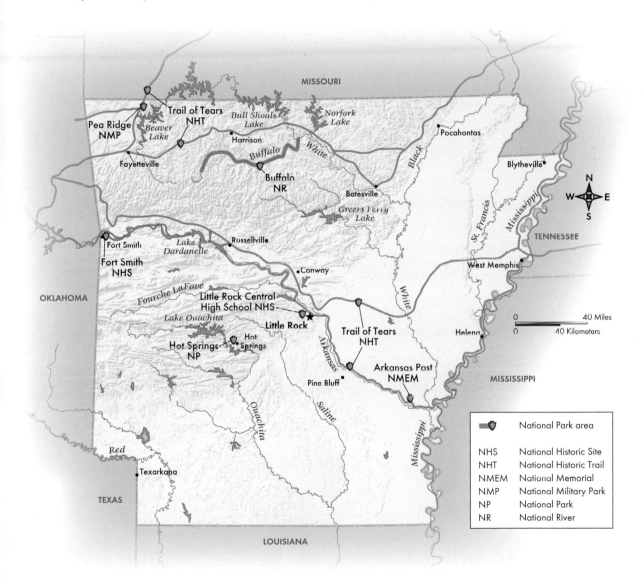

	National Park area
NHS	National Historic Site
NHT	National Historic Trail
NMEM	National Memorial
NMP	National Military Park
NP	National Park
NR	National River

READ ABOUT

Early Native people of Arkansas fishing and bringing back food from a hunt

c. 10,000 BCE

The first humans arrive in what is now Arkansas

▲ **c. 8,000 BCE**
Mammoths (above) and mastodons become extinct

500 BCE

People begin to farm in what is now Arkansas

C H A P T E R   T W O

FIRST PEOPLE

★

SCIENTISTS THINK THAT HUMANS SET FOOT IN NORTH AMERICA AS MUCH AS 20,000 YEARS AGO. During the last ice age, sea levels were lower than they are today, and a section of land between present-day Alaska and Russia peeked above water. People walked across this land to North America to hunt. Over the years, people gradually spread across the continent, arriving in what is now Arkansas about 12,000 years ago.

Caddoan pottery

c. 650 CE

The Plum Bayou culture thrives

800

The Mississippian culture develops

c. 1000 ►

The Caddo culture emerges in southwestern Arkansas

An archaeological dig at Grandview Prairie

WORDS TO KNOW

archaeologists *people who study the remains of past human societies*

artifacts *items created by humans, usually for a practical purpose*

THE EARLIEST ARKANSANS

In Arkansas, the descendants of these Asian hunters found a land with a mild climate. The forests teemed with animals both large and small. **Archaeologists** have found little evidence of the people who first settled Arkansas. But by looking at **artifacts** discovered in nearby states, they can imagine how the first Arkansans lived.

Archaeologists believe that these early people lived in groups of about 20 to 50 people. They lived in simple, temporary structures built from trees, bark, grasses, and other plants, and they moved their camps often. Early Arkansans traveled mostly on foot.

They fed themselves by hunting mammals, using pointed darts that could be launched from curved sticks. The mastodons, mammoths, giant beavers, and other large animals that they hunted became extinct about 10,000 years ago. These early Arkansans also gathered fruit, nuts, berries, and other plants to add to their diet.

After the large mammals became extinct, people began hunting bison, elk, deer, bears, and smaller mammals. These animals provided more than food. People used the skins for clothing and made tools from the horns and bones. These early people used almost every part of the animals that they hunted.

Over the years, the way of life of early Arkansans changed. Groups began settling down in one place or moving around in a smaller area. By 2,500 years ago, people throughout Arkansas had started to farm. They planted squash, sunflowers, and other plants. Populations grew rapidly as farms became more common. People began making pottery, which they used to store seeds and crops. Meanwhile, a variety of cultures developed in Arkansas.

THE MOUND BUILDERS

About 5,000 years ago, some groups living in the highlands west of the Mississippi River began building mounds. Mounds were commonly used for religious ceremonies and community events.

A site called Poverty Point in what is now northeast Louisiana was the center of a powerful and complex mound-building society. Its traders traveled to the Ouachita Mountains to exchange tools, jewelry, and other objects for quartz crystal and other minerals.

The mound-building societies in Arkansas were not as big and powerful as the one at Poverty Point. The Toltec site near present-day Little Rock was the largest. The people who lived there became known as the Plum Bayou culture. Beginning about 650 CE, the Plum Bayou people controlled central Arkansas. Only political and religious leaders and their families lived at the Toltec site. Everyone else lived in permanent villages scattered

FAQ

Q: **WHAT CAUSED THE EXTINCTION OF LARGE MAMMALS SUCH AS THE MAMMOTH?**

A: Some scientists believe that the mammoth (below) and mastodon became extinct because humans overhunted them. Others believe that as the climate warmed, the plants that these large animals ate died out, and the animals soon died as well.

SEE IT HERE!

TOLTEC MOUNDS
ARCHEOLOGICAL STATE PARK

At Toltec Mounds Archeological State Park visitors learn about the Plum Bayou culture and see the state's tallest remaining Native mounds. The park also serves as a research station. Scientists and students study the site to learn more about the Plum Bayou culture.

throughout the area. By 1050, however, they had abandoned the Toltec site. The reason remains unknown, though experts believe that war, disease, or environmental issues could have been the cause.

Native American Peoples
(Before European Contact)

This map shows the general area of Native American peoples before European settlers arrived.

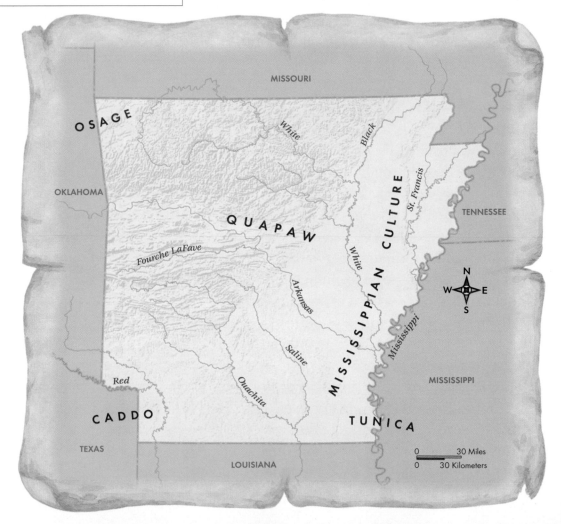

THE MISSISSIPPIAN CULTURE

As Native peoples in Arkansas became highly skilled farmers, they settled into more permanent villages. They relied less on hunting and gathering for their food. They also began trading more often with other bands. People in Arkansas may have traded with groups living as far east as the Carolinas. The bow and arrow, which was adopted in Arkansas around 700 CE, was originally one such trade item. Bows and arrows made hunting much easier. They also made warfare more deadly and more common. Native people built their bows using limbs from Osage orange trees. Archaeologists believe that the first **fortified** villages in Arkansas were built at about the same time that arrow points arrived.

The growth of agriculture and the increased threat of warfare led to a new way of life for many Arkansans. Small settlements grew into large villages. These villages signaled the rise of the Mississippian culture. From 800 to 1600, the peoples living in the Mississippi River valley

WORD TO KNOW

fortified *strengthened by forts or other protective measures*

Archaeologists have found Mississippian village sites from Florida to Oklahoma and north to Wisconsin.

SEE IT HERE!

PARKIN ARCHEOLOGICAL STATE PARK

Parkin Archeological State Park preserves mounds and artifacts from Casqui, a large Mississippian village that was inhabited from about 1000 to 1550. Casqui is the best-preserved Mississippian village in Arkansas. You can tour the site to see the large platform mound and moat. You can also watch archaeologists unearth more clues about the people who once lived here.

belonged to some of the most complex societies that have ever existed in North America.

The typical Mississippian village had a central plaza, which often included a mound. The plaza served as a gathering place and a site for religious ceremonies. Homes and other buildings surrounded the plaza. To protect their villages, people dug ditches and built tall fences made of wooden stakes.

As Native societies grew more food and became more prosperous, a new social structure arose. Each town organized itself into two groups: the elites and the commoners. The elites consisted of a small number of people belonging to the same family. Elites were believed to be descended from the gods and to have supernatural powers. They lived in larger houses, wore special clothes, and ate different food from commoners. They performed religious duties but did not do any of the everyday work. Commoners grew all the food and served as warriors and workers. They also made tools, jewelry, baskets, and pottery.

THE CADDO CULTURE

Around 1000, a different culture arose along the Red River and other waterways in southwestern Arkansas. Like the Mississippians, the Caddo people were farmers. Their settlements, however, were very different. Few Caddos lived in villages. Most lived on small farms that were home to several related families.

Caddos lived in large, round, grass houses 20 feet (6 m) to 50 feet (15 m) across and from 15 feet (4.6 m) to 50 feet (15 m) high. Two or more families lived together in the larger houses. Caddos carved canoes from tree trunks. They also built mounds, which became centers for religious ceremonies and for socializing. Families from around the region would gather at these mounds.

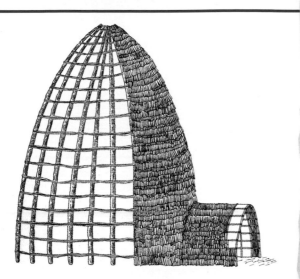

This illustration shows a partially constructed Caddo house.

Picture Yourself . . .

Building a Caddo House

You rise in the morning. It is an exciting day. Today, you are going to help build a grass house. First, you chop down young trees and cut off the branches to make the trunks into long poles. Then you dig holes or a long trench in the ground in the shape of a circle. Next, you arrange the poles in the holes or trench, carefully making sure that all of the poles meet at the top. You weave tree branches between the poles to create a framework shaped like a beehive. As you weave the branches, you leave some areas open to form a door. You don't worry about leaving a hole to allow smoke from your cooking fire to escape, because the smoke will go through the walls.

Now it is time to make the walls of your house. You cut armloads of long grasses or reeds. You weave them tightly together to make thick bundles, called thatch. You start at the bottom, attaching the thatch to the wooden framework. As you work your way up, you overlap the bundles of thatch so that rainwater will run down the side of the house. (Look at the shingles on the roof of a house to see how this works.)

Caddos made pottery with geometric patterns. They also wove baskets and mats out of reeds and grasses. Because they lived on the edge of the Great Plains, some Caddos became bison hunters. These groups acquired horses and moved their camps frequently, following the bison herds.

Caddos often settled near natural salt deposits. Salt was a valuable resource used to flavor food and cure animal hides so they could be worn as clothing. The Caddos gathered the salt and traded it to people located farther away from salt deposits.

CHANGE ON THE HORIZON

By the 1500s, the Native peoples of Arkansas were successful farmers who lived in complex societies. They had established trade relationships with people outside of the region. But the lives of all of these people would change as newcomers crossed the Mississippi.

Caddoan pottery

READ ABOUT

The First
Europeans.....32

French
Arkansas 34

The Louisiana
Purchase.....38

A New
Territory.....40

Early explorers traveled along the coast of North America.

1541
Spanish explorer Hernando de Soto arrives in what is now Arkansas

1682 ▶
René-Robert Cavelier, Sieur de La Salle, claims the Mississippi River basin for France

1686
Arkansas's first permanent European settlement is established at Arkansas Post

CHAPTER THREE

EXPLORATION AND SETTLEMENT

★

SOON AFTER EUROPEANS ARRIVED IN THE AMERICAS IN 1492, SPANISH SHIPS BEGAN EXPLORING THE EASTERN COASTLINE OF NORTH AMERICA. Ship captains hoped to find a water route linking the Atlantic and Pacific oceans. Such a waterway would make it much easier for Europeans to reach their trading partners in Asia. Other Spaniards ventured overland, looking for gold, silver, and other treasures.

1803

With the Louisiana Purchase, Arkansas becomes part of the United States

1804 ▶

William Dunbar (right) and George Hunter lead an expedition through Arkansas

1819

The Arkansas Territory is created

European Exploration of Arkansas

The colored arrows on this map show the approximate routes taken by explorers between 1541 and 1682.

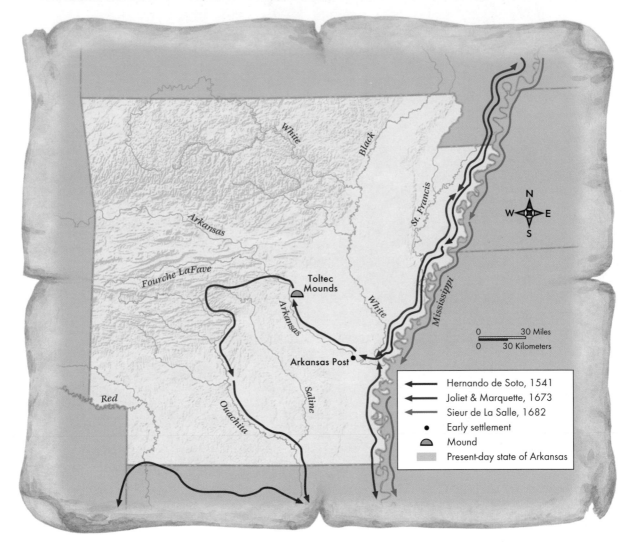

THE FIRST EUROPEANS

An expedition of 400 Spaniards under the command of Hernando de Soto arrived on the eastern banks of the Mississippi River in May 1541. Spain's King Charles I had ordered de Soto to explore North America in the search for gold. The Spaniards had taken unimaginable amounts of gold, silver, and other valuables from the Incan and Aztec peoples of Peru and Mexico, respectively. The king was hungry for more riches. After landing near present-day Tampa, Florida, in 1539, de Soto and his men had roamed across what is now the southern United States. They raided Native villages for food and interpreters. They often captured Native people to carry their gear. De Soto's party ruined crops and burned villages, and they did not find any gold.

It took de Soto two years to reach the Mississippi River. To cross the river, which was 1 mile (1.6 km) wide, de Soto's men spent a month building four large rafts. They loaded about 200 horses and several herds of pigs onto the rafts.

The crude rafts landed on the western shore of the Mississippi River near present-day Helena, Arkansas, in June. De Soto and his men were the first Europeans

The Spaniards brought pigs on the expedition so they would have a reliable source of meat. These pigs are thought to be the ancestors of the Arkansas razorback hogs.

Hernando de Soto's arrival at the Mississippi River in May 1541

MISSISSIPPIAN CHIEF

Casqui (1491?–?) was a Mississippian leader who ruled over a large region in what is now northeastern Arkansas. He met with Hernando de Soto in 1541, soon after the Spaniard's party crossed the Mississippi River. Little is known about Casqui's life, but journals written by de Soto's men describe the peaceful encounter in detail. The journal writers guessed that Casqui was about 50 years old. His house sat atop an earthen mound beside a river. Many archaeologists believe that Casqui's village is part of the present-day Parkin Archeological State Park.

WORDS TO KNOW

colony *a community settled in a new land but with ties to another government*

immunity *natural protection against disease*

missionary *a person who tries to convert others to a religion*

known to set foot in Arkansas. The expedition traveled throughout the area. The Spaniards passed through the wealthy and powerful villages of Pacaha and Casqui in the northeast corner of the state. Later, de Soto caught a fever. He died on May 21, 1542.

The remaining members of the expedition decided to find a land route through Texas to Mexico, which was a Spanish **colony** at the time. However, they were forced to turn back toward Arkansas when they ran low on food and supplies. In 1543, the group built rafts and set sail down the Mississippi River toward the Gulf of Mexico. While traveling, they were frequently attacked by Native people attempting to drive the Spaniards from the region. Only about half of de Soto's original party survived the two-year expedition.

The de Soto expedition had an enormous impact on the region. Some of de Soto's men carried deadly diseases, such as measles and smallpox. Because these diseases had been common in Europe for centuries, many Europeans had built up an **immunity** to them. Native Americans, however, had never before been exposed to these diseases. The diseases quickly spread through the Native villages. So many people in the village of Casqui died that it was abandoned by 1550.

FRENCH ARKANSAS

In 1673, a small group of men arrived at the mouth of the Arkansas River. Led by a French trader, Louis Joliet, and a French **missionary**, Father Jacques Marquette, they had paddled their canoes down the Mississippi River from present-day Illinois. At the point where the Mississippi and Arkansas rivers meet, they stopped at a Quapaw village. The Quapaw people told their visitors that hostile tribes and Spanish settlers would kill the explorers if they continued southward on the Mississippi, and the Frenchmen returned to Illinois.

René-Robert Cavelier, Sieur de La Salle, taking possession of the land at the mouth of the Arkansas River, March 1682

A few years later, French colonist René-Robert Cavelier, Sieur de La Salle, organized an expedition to travel all the way to the mouth of the Mississippi River. La Salle canoed down the Mississippi in 1682 with 22 Frenchmen and 31 Native Americans. The expedition stopped at the Quapaw village of Kappa, near the mouth of the White River. La Salle met with the Indians, who agreed to become trading partners with France. Before leaving Kappa, La Salle erected a large wooden cross and a pole with the coat of arms of France's King Louis XIV. La Salle claimed all the lands of the Mississippi River valley as a colony for France and named the region La Louisiane (French for "land of Louis"), in honor of the French king.

The land that La Salle claimed for France—the Mississippi River valley—covered about one-quarter of the modern United States!

A stovepipe hat made from beaver fur

When de Soto's expedition had explored and devastated Arkansas in the 1540s, it had encountered many villages and towns with large populations. By the time of La Salle's expedition, however, the region had changed dramatically. War and internal arguments had torn apart the powerful Mississippian chiefdoms. Disease had wiped out their villages. Only small groups of Native peoples living in isolated villages remained. Caddos lived in what is now southwestern Arkansas. Quapaws lived along the Mississippi River. Some historians believe the Quapaw people had arrived in Arkansas from farther north after the de Soto expedition passed through. Others believe they are descended from Mississippians. Osages lived in what is now northwestern Arkansas. They were bison hunters whose territory extended into what are now Missouri, Kansas, and Oklahoma.

In Arkansas, the abandoned fields and forests teemed with bison, deer, turkey, otters, beavers, and other wild game. In the years to come, these abundant natural resources would attract newcomers.

In 1686, a member of La Salle's expedition established the first permanent European settlement in Arkansas. Henri de Tonti set up a trading post at the mouth of the Arkansas River. Later known as Arkansas Post, it became the region's fur-trading center. Furs—especially beaver fur—were extremely valuable in Europe at the time. They were used to make fashionable clothes and hats. White traders brought clothes, tools, and weapons to Arkansas Post to swap with Native Americans for furs.

Hearing fantastic stories about the abundant wildlife in Arkansas, French-Canadian hunters made the journey there each winter. They stalked animals, particularly bison and bears. The hunters sent bison meat and bear oil and fat down the Mississippi River to the growing French colonial city of New Orleans. The hunters preserved the bison meat by drying it or salting it. Arkansas's many natural salt springs provided a local source for salt. Local Native Americans taught the hunters how to make oil from bear fat. French colonists used bear oil to make soap, salad dressing, and fuel for their oil lamps.

For more than 100 years, French-Canadian hunters and missionaries often visited Arkansas. Few Europeans settled there permanently, however. By 1800, fewer than 400 non-Indians lived in the region. Most were Spanish, French, and American settlers. Some were enslaved African men and women. Today,

Bison were once abundant on the prairies of Arkansas.

MINI-BIO

HENRI DE TONTI: THE FATHER OF ARKANSAS

Henri de Tonti (1649?–1704) was born in Italy and was a member of La Salle's 1682 expedition to the Mississippi River valley. As a young man, he had lost his hand in a battle in Italy. He attached an iron hook to his arm and later became known as "Iron Hand" to Native Americans. He set up a fur-trading post at the mouth of the Arkansas River and named the settlement Poste de Arkansea (or Arkansas Post). Tonti visited the trading post several times but never returned after 1690. He died of yellow fever in what is now Alabama. Because he established the first European settlement in the state, he gained a new nickname: the Father of Arkansas.

? Want to know more? Visit www.factsfornow.scholastic.com and enter the keyword **Arkansas**.

descendants of French traders and Quapaw women are called métis people, meaning people of mixed European and Native American ancestry. Cordial relations between the traders and the Quapaw were important to French survival in the region.

THE LOUISIANA PURCHASE

In the 1700s, Great Britain, France, and Spain were competing for control of North America and the lucrative fur trade. In 1754, France and Great Britain began battling each other in the French and Indian War. Before the French lost in 1763, they **ceded** Louisiana to Spain so that Britain would not claim it. Spanish officials, however, showed little interest in Arkansas or the rest of the colony.

WORD TO KNOW

ceded *gave up or granted*

Many pioneers traveled to the Mississippi Valley to start new lives.

Spanish control of Arkansas lasted only 37 years. Spain returned the territory to France in 1800, but it would not remain under French rule for long.

By this time, British colonies on the East Coast had declared their independence and become the United States of America. In early 1803, U.S. president Thomas Jefferson sent James Monroe and Robert Livingston to France. Jefferson authorized them to buy New Orleans from the French for $10 million. He believed that the growing port city could be a key part of the young nation's future.

The French had experienced many troubles with their North American colonies. For example, a massive slave revolt drove the French out of Haiti, one of their colonies in the Caribbean. So French officials instead offered Monroe a shocking deal. They would sell the United States the entire Louisiana Territory—much of the land west of the Mississippi River to the Rocky Mountains—for $15 million. Monroe quickly agreed. In April, France and the United States signed a treaty transferring 828,000 square miles (2,145,000 sq km) to the United States. The Louisiana Purchase, as it became known, doubled the size of the country.

President Jefferson charged Meriwether Lewis and William Clark with the job of leading an expedition to explore the northern reaches of the Louisiana Purchase. He gave William Dunbar and George Hunter the task of exploring what are now Arkansas and Louisiana.

Louisiana Purchase

This map shows the area (in yellow) that made up the Louisiana Purchase, which included the present-day state of Arkansas (in orange).

British Possessions

Louisiana Purchase

N W E S

Spanish Possessions

- ▮ United States, 1803
- ▯ Louisiana Purchase
- ▨ United States Territory, 1803
- ▮ Present-day state of Arkansas

FAQ

Q8 HOW MUCH DID THE UNITED STATES AGREE TO PAY PER ACRE IN THE LOUISIANA PURCHASE?

A8 About 3 cents per acre (7 cents per hectare). That's about 61 cents per acre ($1.42 per ha) in today's money.

Explorer William Dunbar

The New Madrid Earthquake, one of the strongest earthquakes ever recorded in the United States, hit New Madrid, Missouri, near northeastern Arkansas, in 1812. It leveled forests but killed few people because the region was sparsely settled.

Dunbar and Hunter's 19-member party, which included two enslaved Africans, began its journey in October 1804. They explored the Red, Black, and Ouachita rivers and studied the interactions between Native Americans and European trappers, traders, and settlers. They also described landscapes, plants, and animals and made the first scientific maps of the region.

Fewer than 500 white settlers had moved to Arkansas while it was under French and Spanish control, though significant numbers of Cherokees moved to the area during this period. The Louisiana Purchase changed everything. Land-hungry people in the eastern states suddenly wanted to move to the country's new territory. A steady stream of white settlers began flowing into Arkansas. The town of Hot Springs was established in 1807. Five years later, the original settlers of Little Rock started building their new homes. Fort Smith was established in 1817. But much of the Arkansas region was too rugged to travel through, much less settle, and large swaths of it remained sparsely populated.

By the time Arkansas became part of the United States, few Native Americans lived in the territory. The Quapaw population had plunged to about 700. The Caddo people had moved into what is now Louisiana and Texas. Many Osage people had moved into what is now Missouri and Oklahoma, though the Osage continued to claim winter hunting lands in northern and northwestern Arkansas.

A NEW TERRITORY

Arkansas was originally part of the Louisiana Territory. As this huge territory was divided into smaller territories, Arkansas eventually became part of the Missouri Territory. When Missouri applied for statehood, its leaders did not believe it was possible for a state government to control such a large territory. They asked Congress to divide the region into smaller parts. On March 2, 1819, President James Monroe signed the act creating the Arkansas Territory. Arkansas Post was named as its capital. The territory had clearly defined northern, eastern, and southern borders. Its western end, however, had no boundary, stretching into the lands of present-day Oklahoma. Arkansas would remain on the western frontier of the United States for many years.

The same year that Arkansas became a territory, a printer named William E. Woodruff arrived at Arkansas Post. On November 20, 1819, he put out the first issue of the territory's first newspaper, the *Arkansas Gazette*. When the territory's capital moved from Arkansas Post to Little Rock in 1821, Woodruff packed up his printing presses and moved there. The *Gazette* became influential in Arkansas politics and society.

In the 1820s, more settlers came to Arkansas. Families built homes, merchants set up businesses, and cotton farms and sawmills sprang up. In 1822, the first steamboat arrived in Arkansas. Steamboats became important in Arkansas because the territory had many rivers and few roads. Arkansas's first major road was called the Southwest Trail. It was a network of dirt routes that ran from the northeast corner of the territory to its southwest corner. Many pioneers traveling to Texas used the Southwest Trail, and some decided that they liked Arkansas and stayed. A second road ran from Memphis, Tennessee, to Little Rock and was later extended to reach Fort Smith. By 1830, Arkansas had a population of more than 30,000. Arkansas had become a growing territory heading toward statehood.

The *Arkansas Gazette* was the oldest newspaper west of the Mississippi River for decades. The paper was printed for more than 170 years before shutting down in 1991.

William E. Woodruff, founder of the *Arkansas Gazette*

42

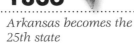

READ ABOUT

A group of immigrants at an Arkansas camp, mid-1800s

1836
Arkansas becomes the 25th state

1830s
Native Americans are forced out of Arkansas

▲**1840s–50s**
The cotton industry flourishes

GROWTH AND CHANGE

★

B Y THE MID-1830s, ARKANSAS WAS HOME TO MORE THAN 40,000 WHITE SETTLERS AND ENSLAVED AFRICANS. Arkansas's population was large enough that it could ask Congress to make it a state. Becoming a state, however, was no easy task.

1861

Arkansas secedes from the United States; it is readmitted in 1868

1868 ►

Powell Clayton is elected governor of Arkansas

1890s

Laws are passed to establish legal segregation

Arkansas: From Territory to Statehood
(1819–1836)

This map shows the original Arkansas territory (outlined in red) and the area (in yellow) that became the state of Arkansas in 1836.

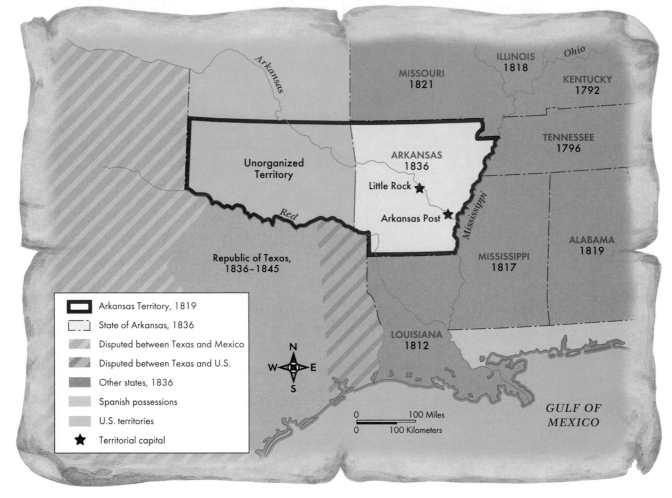

THE SLAVERY DEBATE

Soon after the Louisiana Purchase, the issue of whether slavery would be allowed in the western territories began to be hotly debated. In the Missouri Compromise of 1820, members of Congress prohibited slavery above the latitude of 36°30' north, except for the planned state of Missouri. Arkansas's northern border is at this exact latitude. In

1821, when Missouri was admitted to the Union as a Slave State, Maine joined the Union as a Free State. This kept the number of Slave States and Free States equal. It would be 15 years before another territory became a state.

STATEHOOD

In 1836, the Michigan Territory asked to join the United States. It would be a Free State. Arkansas's leaders knew that Congress would want to admit a Slave State at the same time, so they quickly requested statehood. On June 15, 1836, Arkansas joined the Union as the 25th state. Little Rock was named its capital.

In writing the state's **constitution**, territorial leaders used the U.S. Constitution and the constitutions of other southern states as models. The Arkansas Constitution gave white men the right to vote and legalized slavery. It allowed voters to elect the governor, legislators, and county officials.

From 1835 to 1840, the population of Arkansas nearly doubled, from about 52,000 to almost 100,000. This rapid growth had a major impact on the Native American population. The U.S. government and local officials pressured the Quapaw, Osage, and Caddo groups to surrender their lands. Many moved to the Kansas Territory.

At the same time, the U.S. government began forcing the few Native American nations remaining in the southeastern United States to move to Indian Territory, land the U.S. government set aside in present-day Oklahoma for Native American relocation. About 21,000 Muscogees (or Creeks), 12,500 Choctaws, 6,000 Chickasaws, and 4,200 Seminoles crossed Arkansas on the way to their new land. In 1838, the Cherokee people, the last Native American nation in the Southeast, were forced to leave their homes in Georgia and the Carolinas. They, too, crossed Arkansas on

WORD TO KNOW

constitution *a written document that contains all the governing principles of a state or country*

Enslaved people often lived in groups of cabins on Arkansas plantations.

Cotton bolls

the way to the Indian Territory. More than 4,000 Cherokee men, women, and children died during the forced march, which became known as the Trail of Tears.

After Arkansas became a state, many cotton planters began settling along the state's rivers, especially the Mississippi, Arkansas, and Ouachita. By 1840, a plantation society arose in the southern and eastern parts of the state. The planters brought almost 20,000 enslaved African men and women with them to Arkansas. Enslaved workers drained swamps to create more land suitable for growing cotton. They planted and tended the cotton plants and then harvested, cleaned, and packed the cotton for shipment. Others cleared land for homes and small farms, or worked as blacksmiths, house servants, and cooks.

The slave population in Arkansas grew steadily. Slaves made up 11 percent of the state's population in 1820, 20 percent in 1840, and peaked at 26 percent in 1860. Most enslaved workers in Arkansas lived on plantations. They were forced to work hard, live in simple cabins, and endure harsh and sometimes violent treatment. Some slaves lived in Little Rock and other towns, working as craftspeople and household servants. Enslaved Africans tried to escape whenever they could. Nelson Hackett served as a butler for a wealthy Arkansan in Washington County. He managed to steal a racehorse and ride all the way to Canada and freedom.

For most of Arkansas's white population, times were good in the 1840s and 1850s. Arkansas's cotton industry boomed during this period as cotton production declined in areas such as Virginia and Georgia. In those states, so much cotton had been produced for so long that the soil was worn out. In Arkansas, cotton grew well in the rich soil of the river bottomlands, and planters used the rivers to transport their crops to market.

Meanwhile, new towns and businesses sprang up. Steamboats and wagons brought goods and people into the state. Farmers cut down forests to make fields. Mines produced coal, iron, and lead. Agriculture dominated the state's economy. Although cotton was the most valuable crop, small farms also produced wheat, oats, corn, and tobacco. Farmers raised cows, pigs, and other livestock as well. Even as part of Arkansas prospered, many western areas remained a wild, barely populated frontier.

TIME OF WAR

Slavery in the South and its expansion into the western territories became a major issue in the 1860 presidential election. Northern states had outlawed slavery several decades earlier. Planters and politicians in Southern states, however, were determined to keep the profitable plantation system and slavery in place. Although rich planters made up only a small portion of the population in Arkansas, they controlled the state's government and commerce. They fought to maintain the slavery system.

SEE IT HERE!

HISTORIC ARKANSAS MUSEUM

At the Historic Arkansas Museum in Little Rock, you can see the Pemberton family's 1850s farmstead. The buildings were moved from their original location near Scott, just east of Little Rock. The restored farmstead includes the main house, barn, and slave cabin. You can see how the enslaved workers on the Pemberton farm lived.

47

Although many other Confederate states had larger populations than Arkansas, Arkansas provided more troops for the Union army than all but one other Confederate state.

WORD TO KNOW

secede *to withdraw from a group or organization*

A scene from the Battle of Pea Ridge, March 1862

When Abraham Lincoln ran for president in 1860, election officials in Southern slaveholding states refused to include his name on ballots. Lincoln was elected anyway, and these states began to **secede** from the United States because they feared that he would outlaw slavery. By February 1, 1861, seven Southern states had left the Union to form the Confederate States of America (CSA).

Arkansas held a convention in March 1861 to decide whether to secede. The delegates rejected secession in a close vote. But on the East Coast, there was no turning back. In April 1861, Confederates fired on Fort Sumter, a Union fort in South Carolina. The Civil War had begun.

The start of the war changed the minds of some Arkansans over the issue of secession. Delegates met again in May, and this time they voted 69–1 to secede. Arkansas left the Union and joined the CSA.

Around 60,000 young Arkansans joined the Confederate army. Many residents in the northern mountains, where there were few slaves or slaveholders, remained loyal to the United States. About 9,000 white Arkansans joined the Union army, along with about 5,000 black Arkansans, some of them former slaves.

The largest battle to take place in Arkansas during the Civil War was the Battle of Pea Ridge in March 1862, in which Union forces defeated the Confederates, forcing them back to Mississippi. Other battles took place in major towns along transportation routes into the state and at several strategic points along the Mississippi River on Arkansas's eastern border.

On July 4, 1863, Confederate troops launched an attack on a Union stronghold in Helena. The Confederates were defeated. On the same day, the key Confederate fort at Vicksburg, Mississippi, had surrendered. The Union now controlled most of the Mississippi River. By August, Arkansas's Confederate government had left the state capital for Washington in the southwestern part of the state. It served as the capital of the state's Confederate government for the rest of the war. Much of the state became a "no man's land" where no government or military held control. Union troops took possession of Little Rock with almost no resistance.

MINI-BIO

DAVID OWEN DODD: A CONFEDERATE HERO

Seventeen-year-old David Owen Dodd (1846–1864) left Union-occupied Little Rock after a short visit. Union soldiers stopped him. They discovered that his notebook had pages written in Morse code. The dots and dashes were decoded. The pages contained details about the location of Union troops. Dodd was found guilty of spying and sentenced to die. A Union general offered to free him if he revealed who had given him the information. According to legend, Dodd replied, "I can die for my country, but I cannot betray the trust of a friend." He was hanged on January 8, 1864, and buried at Little Rock's Mount Holly Cemetery. Near his grave is a marble monument etched with the words, "Boy Martyr of the Confederacy."

Want to know more? Visit www.factsfornow.scholastic.com and enter the keyword **Arkansas**.

WORD TO KNOW

martyr *a person who dies for his or her beliefs*

50

The Civil War continued for nearly two more years. Finally, in April 1865, the CSA surrendered. The Union had won the war.

RECONSTRUCTION

The Civil War devastated Arkansas. More than 10,000 Arkansans lost their lives. Many others were wounded. Returning war veterans found their farms and businesses destroyed. Some once-populated areas were left entirely empty of people. African Americans celebrated their freedom, but most found themselves without homes, jobs, and money. The war created a bleak and resentful mood that would last for decades.

The U.S. government provided money and other aid to southern states to reorganize their governments and to help people rebuild their lives. This period is known as Reconstruction. The most visible federal agency was the Bureau of Refugees, Freedmen, and Abandoned Lands, which was also called the Freedmen's Bureau. It helped educate people who had been released from slavery and negotiated labor contracts for them.

Plantation owners had lots of land, but they no longer had enslaved workers. Throughout the South, a new economic arrangement arose called sharecropping. A landowner provided a plot of land for a sharecropper to farm, along with seeds, tools, food, and housing. The sharecropper would plant seeds, tend the crops, and harvest them.

Farmworkers in Arkansas present a peanut crop for inspection, 1899.

When the harvest was finished, the landowner figured out the sharecropper's earnings for that growing season. From this amount, he deducted half (or more) for the use of his land. He also deducted the cost of food, housing, and farm supplies.

Landowners often cheated sharecroppers by paying such low prices for the crops or charging so much for the supplies that the sharecroppers received nothing at the end of the year. No matter how hard sharecroppers worked, they stayed in debt. Sharecropping was not limited to black families. Many white families also worked as sharecroppers.

In the 1866 elections, Arkansas voters returned many former Confederates to office. Conflicts soon arose with U.S. officials when these politicians passed laws to restrict the freedoms of black Arkansans. Like other southern states, Arkansas refused to give African Americans full citizenship rights. In 1867, Congress stepped in, assigning military officers to govern the former Confederate states. Congress required these states to adopt new constitutions that would recognize the citizenship rights of black men.

In January 1868, 70 delegates, including eight African Americans, met in Little Rock. They drafted a document that gave black men the right to vote and prohibited the state from denying any American male citizenship rights "on account of race, color, or previous servitude." At the time, former Confederate soldiers and officials were not allowed to vote in Arkansas without first taking an oath of loyalty to the United States. Many of these people, who made up the majority of white voters in the state, refused to take the oath. As a result, Arkansas voters approved the new constitution easily, and Arkansas was soon readmitted to the Union.

Conditions improved for some African Americans. Mifflin Gibbs, an African American, was elected a judge in Little Rock in 1873. Soon the city had three black colleges. But while the new constitution gave African American men the basic rights of citizenship, in reality, they were often persecuted. Black men, women, and children faced daily hostility and frequent violence. Secret organizations, such as the Ku Klux Klan (KKK), intimidated, attacked, and murdered them throughout the South. By the early 1900s, more than 200 African Americans in Arkansas had been lynched—killed by a mob without a trial.

During the 1890s, the Arkansas legislature passed laws establishing **segregation** and preventing African Americans from exercising their **civil rights**. By law, African Americans had to sit in separate railroad cars from white passengers. They had to use separate doors to enter theaters. Another law prevented African Americans from voting in Democratic primary elections. (At the time, Democrats won almost all the important elections in the

FAQ

Q8 WHERE DID THE NAME JIM CROW COME FROM?

A8 Jim Crow was the name of a black character portrayed by a white performer in the 1830s. The character would dance, sing, and smile, and whites used him to ridicule African Americans.

WORDS TO KNOW

segregation *separation from others, according to race, class, ethnic group, religion, or other factors*

civil rights *basic human rights that all citizens in a society are entitled to, such as the right to vote*

state.) This system of segregation, known as Jim Crow, separated Arkansas into two societies: one white and the other black—one privileged and the other oppressed.

POVERTY AND PROGRESS

By 1890, railroads crisscrossed most of Arkansas. They brought people and goods into the state and carried Arkansas's timber, coal, and other raw materials to buyers around the country. The railroad companies also encouraged fruit farmers. Thriving apple orchards and strawberry fields arose in northwestern Arkansas. The railroads wanted more business, so they published advertisements in Europe about land opportunities in Arkansas. People from Germany, Slovakia, and other countries immigrated to the state and became fruit farmers.

In the late 1800s, railroads, such as this one along Spring River, began transporting goods across the state.

79000 SPRING RIVER NEAR HARDY, ARK. "ON THE FRISCO"

FRED HARVEY

PRESERVING CHEROKEE HERITAGE

Mabel Washbourne Anderson helped preserve her people's heritage by writing articles and books about Cherokee history, art, and ways of life. She was born in Arkansas and graduated from Oklahoma's Cherokee Female Seminary in 1883. She taught in public schools in Oklahoma. She began writing articles for local newspapers in the 1890s. She is best known for her biography of Stand Watie, a Cherokee who served as a general in the Confederate army during the Civil War.

Business owners and workers inside the Southern Mercantile Company in Pine Bluff, 1902

Because the railroads could bring in food products from other states, many eastern Arkansas farmers began focusing on cash crops (those that were mostly sold for profit), particularly cotton. Between 1879 and 1899, the amount of farmland in the state devoted to cotton soared from 29 percent to 57 percent.

During this period, many of the state's African Americans were on the move. The adoption of machinery on cotton farms put many black farm laborers out of work. Some moved to Arkansas's growing cities to find work. Many, however, packed up their belongings and left the state. African Americans from all across the South soon moved to cities in the North and West to find better jobs and to escape harassment and segregation. This is known as the Great Migration. Some of those who remained in Arkansas became successful farmers and businesspeople, creating a small black middle class.

Meanwhile, Arkansas's cities were growing. New banks, hotels, restaurants, and theaters sprang up in the cities. Arkansas Industrial University (now the University of Arkansas) was founded in Fayetteville in 1872. Eight students, including one woman, were enrolled.

Despite this progress, Arkansas remained one of the country's poorest states for nearly a century after the Civil War. Many farmers and farmworkers remained stuck in poverty. By 1900, 70 percent of the jobs were still on farms. Industrialization lagged behind other states. The state had difficulty raising enough money from taxes, and its educational system and transportation networks were poor compared to much of the nation.

During the first two decades of the 20th century, economic conditions improved slightly in Arkansas. Lumber and mining industries blossomed. Mines near Little Rock produced bauxite, the ore refined into aluminum.

Then, in 1917, the United States entered World War I. About 70,000 Arkansans fought in the war, which was already raging in Europe. When the war ended in 1918, Arkansas's soldiers returned home, ready to get back to work.

THE WILD WEST IN ARKANSAS

During the late 1800s and early 1900s, Texarkana and Fort Smith became notorious for gambling, alcohol drinking, and even gunfights. These towns were like the legendary Wild West towns. Religious and women's groups worked to stop these activities, which they believed harmed society and families. Activist Carrie Nation so hated alcohol that she sometimes smashed up saloons where it was sold. She was frequently arrested in Arkansas and neighboring states. Eventually, some cities and counties outlawed gambling and saloons.

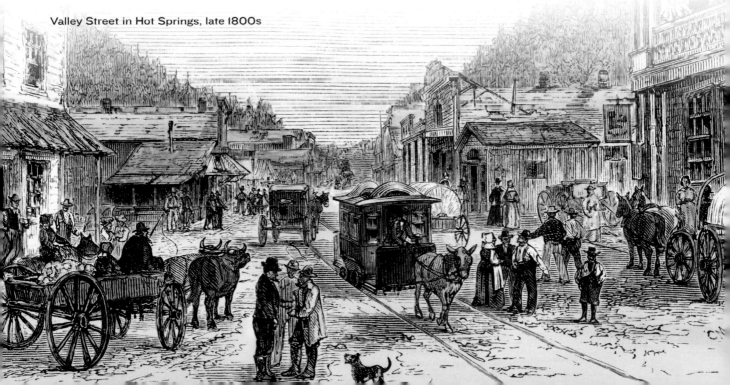

Valley Street in Hot Springs, late 1800s

56

READ ABOUT

A busy Little Rock street, early 1900s

1919

Hundreds of African Americans are killed in Phillips County

1930

A drought strikes Arkansas

1932 ▶

Hattie Wyatt Caraway becomes the first woman elected to the U.S. Senate

CHAPTER FIVE

MORE MODERN TIMES

★

IN THE YEARS AFTER WORLD WAR I, THE AMERICAN ECONOMY BOOMED. U.S. companies produced more than ever, and many new businesses started up. Companies began paying workers higher wages, so more Americans had money to buy the newfangled goods that were being sold. They bought cars and radios and went out to the movies. It was the Roaring Twenties, and to many Americans, life seemed good.

1957
Violence erupts when
Little Rock tries to
desegregate its schools

1981 ▶
Charles Bussey
becomes mayor of
Little Rock

2010
Flash floods kill 20
people at Albert Pike
Recreation Area

An oil well blows near El Dorado, January 10, 1921.

GOOD TIMES, TROUBLED TIMES

Some Arkansans joined in this national prosperity. In 1921, oil was discovered near El Dorado in southern Arkansas. Within four years, the town's population soared from 4,000 to 30,000. But Arkansas did not enjoy the same prosperity in the Roaring Twenties as some other states. Few new factories or industries started during the decade. The state's economy remained based primarily on agriculture, and many farmers struggled to make ends meet. Poverty still gripped many rural areas, and Arkansas remained one of the country's poorest states.

Life was particularly difficult for Arkansas's African Americans, who had long been victims of harassment and violence. In the early 20th century, the white residents of Harrison and many other towns in northern and western Arkansas forced all black residents to move away. These towns became known as "sundown towns," because African Americans were warned that they would be killed if they stayed in town past dark.

In 1919, violence exploded in Phillips County in the eastern part of the state. Black farmers were meeting to discuss forming a union. An argument outside the meeting left a white man dead, igniting what came to be known as the Elaine Massacre. A false rumor spread that the county's African Americans were staging an uprising. For three days, mobs of whites attacked black citizens. Governor Charles Brough called in federal troops to calm the violence. It is estimated that several hundred African Americans were killed by the mobs. Then in 1927, an African American named John Carter was lynched after being accused of assault. Afterward, thousands of whites rioted, and tensions remained high for weeks.

Meanwhile, Arkansas women were fighting for their right to vote. In 1917, the Arkansas general assembly passed a law giving women the right to vote in primary (but not in general) elections. Two years later, Arkansas ratified the Nineteenth Amendment to the U.S. Constitution, which gave women across the country the right to vote. The amendment was made official in 1920. In 1932, Arkansan Hattie Wyatt Caraway became the first woman elected to the U.S. Senate.

HARD TIMES

In April 1927, floodwaters swamped Arkansas. The flood ruined crops, swept away houses, and destroyed entire towns. More than 750,000 Arkansans lost their homes, their possessions, and their jobs.

MINI-BIO

HATTIE WYATT CARAWAY: PIONEERING SENATOR

Hattie Wyatt Caraway (1878–1950) was the first woman ever elected to the U.S. Senate. Born in Tennessee, she moved to Jonesboro with her husband in 1902. A popular politician, Thaddeus Caraway served in the U.S. House of Representatives (1913–1921) and the U.S. Senate (1921–1931). After he died in 1931, Hattie Caraway won a special election to fill the empty seat. Arkansas voters reelected her in 1938, and she served in the Senate until 1945.

Want to know more? Visit www.factsfornow.scholastic.com and enter the keyword **Arkansas**.

During the 1927 flood, the Mississippi River swelled to 60 miles (97 km) wide in some places!

As Arkansans slowly began to recover from the flood, another natural disaster struck. During the spring and summer of 1930, little rain fell throughout the state. This drought came during the most important part of the growing season. Farmers watched their crops wither. With no plants to hold the rich topsoil in place, winds simply blew it away. Many Arkansas farmers gave up. They packed up all their belongings and left the state. Most headed to California and other western states, hoping to find a better life. The farmers who stayed behind struggled to feed their families.

To make matters even worse, the United States had plunged into an economic collapse called the Great Depression. Agriculture and other areas of the economy were already doing poorly when a panic wrecked the nation's financial markets in October 1929. Millions of people sold their **stocks**, causing prices to plunge. Banks closed as too many people tried to withdraw their money. Many factories and businesses throughout the country shut their doors.

By 1933, 15 million of the country's 50 million workers were unemployed. Meanwhile, farmers suffered as crop prices plunged. For many, life fell apart during the Great Depression. Families were uprooted as people moved around in search of jobs. Soup kitchens fed the hungry and the homeless.

In 1933, Franklin Roosevelt became president, promising to end the Depression. He called his plan the New Deal. The New Deal put many Arkansans back to work. Federal programs hired tens of thousands of Arkansans to build schools, libraries, and roads. They built trails at parks such as Devil's Den near Fayetteville. New Deal programs hired artists to paint murals on the walls of post offices and writers to write about the history of the

A dry riverbed in Little Rock, 1934

state. Other programs hired workers to talk to people who had been born into slavery. This slave narrative project helped keep alive the stories of many former Arkansas slaves. Another federal program helped bring electricity to some parts of rural Arkansas.

Under the New Deal, Arkansas's farmers were paid to grow less cotton. With less cotton for sale, its price increased. From 1932 to 1936, the price of cotton doubled. As the years passed, Arkansas's businesses and farms slowly began to recover.

Japanese Americans dig a drainage ditch at the Rohwer Relocation Camp, where they were held during World War II.

The U.S. Army's 442nd Regimental Combat Team was made up entirely of Japanese American soldiers. They won more medals for bravery in Italy than any other U.S. unit.

A NATION AT WAR

Although the New Deal helped Americans survive the Great Depression, it did not end the economic crisis. The Depression did not end until World War II began in Europe. In 1939, Germany invaded Poland, and Great Britain and France declared war on Germany. Then Japan, an ally of Germany, attacked a U.S. naval base at Pearl Harbor, Hawai'i, in December 1941. The United States joined the war.

After the Pearl Harbor attack, some people were concerned that Japanese Americans might be loyal to Japan rather than the United States. As a result, the U.S. government forced thousands of Japanese American families on the West Coast to leave their homes and live in relocation camps until the war was over. Almost two-thirds of the people imprisoned in these camps were U.S. citizens. In

1942, two of these camps were set up in Arkansas. About 8,500 people lived in each camp, confined behind barbed-wire fences. Some young men from these camps volunteered to fight for the U.S. Army.

More than 200,000 Arkansans served in World War II. The state's aluminum and oil industries boomed, supplying metal and fuel to the military. The U.S. government built six plants in Arkansas to make bombs and rockets, and it established several bases and airfields. The war effort created many jobs for Arkansas workers. With so many people off fighting the war, many women and African Americans had the opportunity to fill these jobs. Women made up 75 percent of the 13,000 workers at a bomb-making factory near Jacksonville. Many of these women stayed in the workforce after the war.

In 1945, Germany and Japan surrendered. The war effort helped to revive Arkansas's economy. After the war, returning soldiers and unemployed farmworkers moved to the state's cities to work in the new factories. In the early 1950s, the state adopted a new nickname, Land of Opportunity, to attract more businesses and industries. Many businesses moved to the southern United States during this period because wages were lower than in the North. Companies such as Reynolds Aluminum set up factories in Arkansas. By 1960, manufacturing made up a larger segment of the state's economy than agriculture.

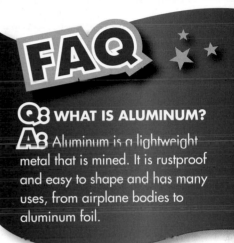

FAQ

Q: WHAT IS ALUMINUM?
A: Aluminum is a lightweight metal that is mined. It is rustproof and easy to shape and has many uses, from airplane bodies to aluminum foil.

THE CIVIL RIGHTS MOVEMENT

Since the Civil War, African Americans throughout the South had been denied their full rights. A legalized system of segregation separated blacks from whites. Black students were not allowed to attend the same schools as white students. Blacks were banned from swimming at public pools, eating at restaurants, and staying at hotels used by whites. They even had to drink from separate water fountains and use separate restrooms. Arkansas's general assembly had passed laws making it difficult for African Americans in Arkansas to vote. For example, only whites could vote in primary elections, and all voters had to pay a $1 poll tax. In addition, election officials often required this tax to be paid at times of the year when poor farm laborers were less likely to have money. Many African Americans (and many whites as well) did not vote because they could not afford to pay the fee.

In the mid-1950s, African Americans began to strongly challenge the laws supporting segregation. They gained support from some white people who were appalled by the **discrimination**. In 1948, the first African American students were admitted to the University of Arkansas's law school and medical school. In 1954, 15 black students enrolled at the University of Arkansas. (African Americans had studied at the university when it first opened in 1872 but were kept out afterward.) Little Rock's bus system was peacefully desegregated in 1956.

Progress in Arkansas's public schools was much slower and rockier. In 1954, the U.S. Supreme Court had ruled in the case of *Brown v. Board of Education of Topeka* (Kansas) that segregation in public schools was illegal. The Court's decision raised hope in African American communities across the country. The same year, three Arkansas school districts voted to desegregate classrooms. Two of the districts ended segregation without any problems. They were the first school districts in the former Confederate states to **integrate**. In the third district, however, the school board reversed its vote to integrate when confronted by angry white parents and citizens. With the segregated schools preserved in that district, most of the town's black families moved away.

WORDS TO KNOW

discrimination *unequal treatment based on race, gender, religion, or other factors*

integrate *to bring together all members of society*

The Little Rock Nine are escorted from Central High School by federal guards in 1957.

In 1957, a federal court ordered Little Rock to integrate its public schools. On September 4, 1957, nine black students tried to attend the previously all-white Little Rock Central High School. These six girls and three boys would become known as the Little Rock Nine. Arkansas governor Orval Faubus opposed integration. He sent the state's National Guard to keep the African American students from entering the school. The federal court, however, ordered Faubus to allow the students to enter the school.

On September 23, the Little Rock Nine entered the school. An unruly mob of about 1,000 white students and adults gathered outside the school. City police removed the black students from the school to prevent a full-scale riot. Television viewers throughout the country watched the events unfold. Little Rock became the bitter face of segregation.

MINI-BIO

DAISY BATES: CIVIL RIGHTS LEADER

Daisy Bates (1914–1999) was the driving force behind the integration of Little Rock schools. Bates and her husband, L. C. Bates, started publishing the Arkansas State Press, a weekly newspaper that called for equal rights, in 1941. She was also the president of the state chapter of the National Association for the Advancement of Colored People (NAACP). In 1956, she became the spokesperson for African Americans seeking to integrate Little Rock's schools. In 2001, the Arkansas general assembly designated the third Monday in February as Daisy Gatson Bates Day in Arkansas.

? Want to know more? Visit www.factsfornow .scholastic.com and enter the keyword **Arkansas**.

President Dwight D. Eisenhower stepped in to resolve the situation. He sent in U.S. Army troops to escort the black students to school. He also removed the Arkansas National Guard from the control of Governor Faubus. On September 25, the students were again allowed in the school. Throughout the school year, white students taunted, hit, and threatened the black students. U.S. Army and Arkansas National Guard soldiers walked the black students to school and monitored the hallways. In May 1958, Ernest Green became the first black graduate of Little Rock Central High School.

The segregationists did not give up without a fight. In September 1958, Little Rock voters chose to close their public high schools rather than integrate them. For an entire year, Little Rock's high schools were closed. During this "Lost Year," many students moved in with relatives in other towns so they could attend school. Others took classes by mail. Some poor students dropped out of school for good. Little Rock public schools did not reopen until September 1959. New school board members were elected, and they supported integrating the schools.

In 1961, civil rights groups in Little Rock pressured city officials to integrate public facilities, such as buildings and parks. Students from Philander Smith College

Students at Arkansas Agricultural, Mechanical, and Normal College (now the University of Arkansas at Pine Bluff) protesting school segregation, 1962

staged **sit-ins** at department store lunch counters. The students were arrested, but business leaders convinced the stores to serve African Americans at the lunch counters. Civil rights volunteers from Arkansas and other states organized a drive to register black voters. These voters helped elect Winthrop Rockefeller governor in 1964 and 1968. Rockefeller worked to improve public schools and promote equal opportunities for all Arkansans. Public schools across Arkansas integrated, but it was a slow process. Some did not integrate until the 1970s.

WORD TO KNOW

sit-ins *acts of protest that involve sitting in seats or on the floor of an establishment and refusing to leave*

The River Market District in downtown
Little Rock

A MODERN STATE

Two Arkansas businesses led an economic revival in the
1980s and 1990s. Based in Springdale, poultry processor
Tyson Foods grew steadily to become the world's largest
processor of chicken and beef. Meanwhile, Walmart, which
began as a small discount department store in Rogers,
expanded to become the world's largest corporation by 2002.

The worldwide financial crisis of 2007–2008 caused a
sharp economic downturn in Arkansas and the rest of the
United States. The real estate market was hit especially
hard, in part because of overbuilding in the previous several
years. Many Arkansas factories relocated to Latin America
and Asia, resulting in severe job losses in the state. Despite

the slump, unemployment remained below the national average in some parts of the state, as new companies moved in and others expanded.

In 2010, Hewlett-Packard, one of the world's largest technology companies, opened a customer service center in Conway that provided jobs for more than 1,200 Arkansas workers. By 2010, six major companies that manufacture parts for wind turbines opened or announced new facilities in Arkansas, creating nearly 3,000 additional jobs in the Little Rock area.

Arkansas has historically been one of the nation's poorest-performing states academically. New programs to improve education, however, are paying off. In 2007, schools received a boost when the Arkansas legislature approved the largest expenditure for education—$456 million—in the state's history. Although Arkansas students continue to perform slightly below the national average, the state ranks near the top in school funding and teacher improvement. The state has also established top-rated systems and standards to ensure higher quality education from kindergarten through high school. These critical reforms will in time result in higher test scores and higher graduation rates by Arkansas students.

Arkansas governor Mike Beebe (left) listens as a Hewlett-Packard representative announces the company's plans to expand its Conway center in 2013.

REACHING AN UNDERSTANDING

On September 4, 1957, teenagers Elizabeth Eckford and Hazel Bryan Massery stood on opposite sides of the confrontation at Central High School. Massery was a white student at Central. That day, she joined the crowd in taunting and jeering Eckford, one of the Little Rock Nine. A widely reproduced photograph showed her shouting at Eckford, who was walking by herself, surrounded by angry white faces. In 1963, Massery contacted Eckford to apologize. Eckford accepted the apology. For a few years in the late 1990s, they gave speeches on racial understanding to students and other groups.

READ ABOUT

Fans celebrate
a victory for the
University of
Arkansas men's
basketball team.

CHAPTER SIX

PEOPLE

★

A NEWLY ARRIVED FAMILY FROM KOREA ATTENDS A PLACE OF WORSHIP IN LITTLE ROCK. An African American lawyer questions a witness at a courthouse in West Memphis. A Mexican American woman opens her grocery store in Springdale. A teenager helps harvest soybeans on a farm in Ashley County that his family has owned for generations. These are just some of the people who call Arkansas home.

Some Arkansas residents, such as this family near Jasper, live in rural areas.

Big City Life

This list shows the population of Arkansas's biggest cities.

Little Rock	193,524
Fort Smith	86,209
Fayetteville	73,580
Springdale	69,797
Jonesboro	67,263

Source: U.S. Census Bureau, 2010 census

CITY AND COUNTRY

Arkansas's major cities are located throughout the state. Little Rock, its largest city, sits almost exactly in the middle of the state. Little Rock and Fort Smith became trading and transportation hubs because they sit on the Arkansas River. As home to Arkansas State University and large food-processing businesses, Jonesboro has become the northeast region's center for education and business. Fayetteville grew because it is home to the University of Arkansas. Springdale's population has soared in the past two decades because it has become the northwest region's transportation hub and the base of the state's poultry industry.

Where Arkansans Live

The colors on this map indicate population density throughout the state.
The darker the color, the more people live there.

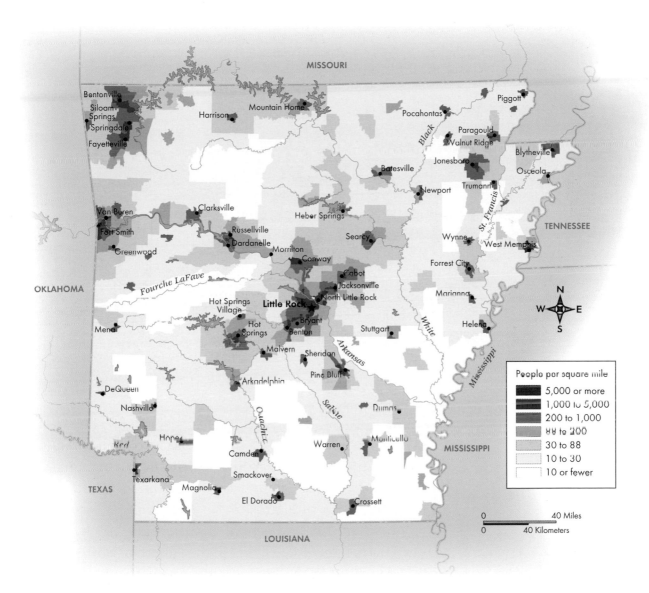

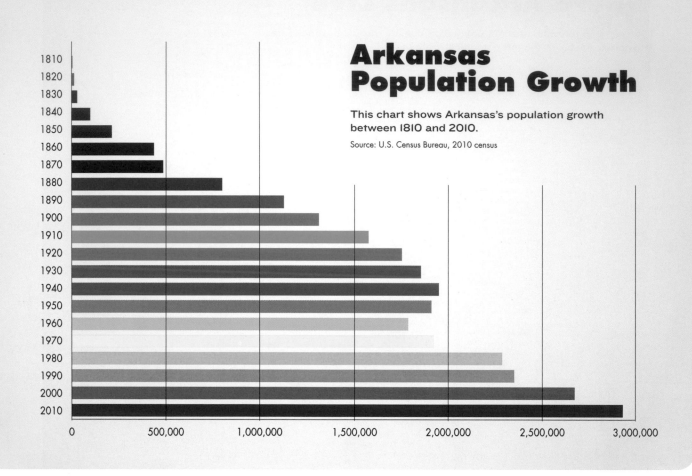

Arkansas Population Growth

This chart shows Arkansas's population growth between 1810 and 2010.

Source: U.S. Census Bureau, 2010 census

What's life like today in Arkansas? It depends on who you are and where you live. About 56 percent of Arkansans make their homes in urban areas. The other 44 percent live in rural areas.

More than 190,000 people live in Little Rock, with another more than 60,000 living in the suburb of North Little Rock. Compared to the biggest cities in most other states, Little Rock isn't very big. It has a slower pace and feels more like a small town. In 2000, nearly half of the state's population lived in communities of 2,500 people or less. Among

People QuickFacts

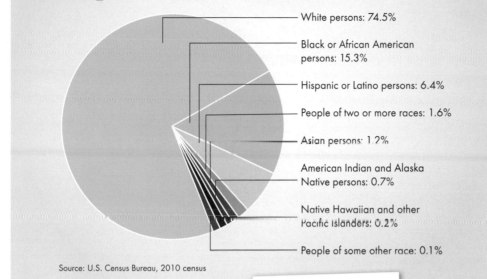

White persons: 74.5%

Black or African American persons: 15.3%

Hispanic or Latino persons: 6.4%

People of two or more races: 1.6%

Asian persons: 1.2%

American Indian and Alaska Native persons: 0.7%

Native Hawaiian and other Pacific Islanders: 0.2%

People of some other race: 0.1%

Source: U.S. Census Bureau, 2010 census

the 50 states, it ranks sixth in terms of highest percentage of state residents who live in rural areas.

DIVERSE PEOPLE

Arkansas is a diverse state. About three-quarters of the population is white. Most are of Irish, German, or English ancestry.

Since the early 1800s, African Americans have made up a significant portion of Arkansas's population. Most African Americans live in the Mississippi Delta region or in the

MINI-BIO

MILTON CRENCHAW: AFRICAN AMERICAN AIRMAN

Milton Crenchaw (1919—) is a flight instructor who taught African American pilots at Alabama's Tuskegee Airfield. Born and raised in Little Rock, he earned his pilot's license in 1941 under a federal program to train black pilots. The Tuskegee Airmen, as they became known, were the first black pilots to serve in the U.S. military. Crenchaw worked as a military flight instructor for 31 years. He also taught aviation at Philander Smith College in Little Rock. He and the other Tuskegee Airmen received the Congressional Gold Medal in 2007.

❓ Want to know more? Visit www.factsfornow .scholastic.com and enter the keyword **Arkansas**.

Drummers play on a Little Rock
sidewalk.

state's larger cities. More than one-quarter of all African Americans in Arkansas live in or near Little Rock.

Hispanics, or Latinos, are the fastest growing ethnic group in Arkansas. The number of Latinos living in the state rose from fewer than 20,000 in 1990 to more than 185,000 in 2010. Most of Arkansas's Latinos trace their origins to Mexico. The growth of the Latino population can be seen in many areas of the state, especially the northwestern corner. Many moved to Arkansas to work in the state's poultry industry, and some have started their own small businesses. Spanish-language radio stations and newspapers, such as *El Latino* and *Noticias Libres*, show the growing influence of Arkansas's Latino residents.

Arkansas's Asian population has also grown a great deal since 1990, rising from about 12,000 in 1990 to just over 35,000 in 2010. Most Asians living in Arkansas trace their heritage to Vietnam, China, India, the Philippines, and the Pacific Islands. Fort Smith is home to sizable Vietnamese and Laotian communities.

Native Americans are central to Arkansas's heritage. Those who live in Arkansas today are most likely to be of Cherokee or Choctaw heritage and live along the western border with Oklahoma.

MINI-BIO

MARGARITA SOLÓRZANO: A COMMUNITY LEADER

Margarita Solórzano (1959–) works as executive director of the Hispanic Women's Organization of Arkansas. She immigrated to the United States in 1990 from Mexico, and she and her two daughters moved to Springdale in 1996. Solórzano earned a degree from North West Arkansas Community College while working at a tortilla factory. Her organiza-tion provides programs that assist Latino immigrants in their new communities and celebrate Latino cultures.

? **Want to know more?** Visit www.facts fornow.scholastic.com and enter the keyword **Arkansas**.

Shoppers browse the fresh flowers at a farmers market in Fayetteville.

A menu in Helena offers country fried steak and other specialties.

HOW TO TALK LIKE AN ARKANSAN

Like many southerners, some Arkansans say "y'all" for the plural form of "you." In a rural area, someone might say they're "fit to be tied after I slipped in the hog wallow." This means they're angry ("fit to be tied") because they fell in the pigpen ("hog wallow"). Don't stick an "Arkansas toothpick" in your mouth. It's a large knife! And if you're watching a University of Arkansas Razorbacks sports team play, be sure to cheer, "Wooo pig sooie!"

HOW TO EAT LIKE AN ARKANSAN

What you eat in Arkansas often depends on where you live. Each region has its own traditional foods. In the southeast, rice dishes (such as Creole shrimp), fresh vegetables, biscuits, and cobbler are a popular meal. Along the Mississippi River, catfish and other fish often end up on the dinner plate. In the Ozarks, bacon and corn bread are everyday foods. In the southwest, Texas-style chili and barbecue are common meals.

MENU

WHAT'S ON THE MENU IN ARKANSAS?

★ ★ ★

Grits

Grits

Grits are small, broken-up grains of corn that are cooked in water until they are soft. They are usually eaten at breakfast but are sometimes served at lunch and dinner.

Fried Catfish

Catfish filets are dunked in a bowl of beaten eggs and then coated with cornmeal and seasonings. Then they are fried in either a skillet or a deep fryer.

Fried Green Tomatoes

Unripe tomato slices are dunked in a bowl of beaten eggs and then coated in cornmeal or flour (or a mixture of both) and seasonings. Then they are fried in a skillet.

Fresh Produce

Arkansas gardens and fields grow a variety of fruits and vegetables. So you can feast on fresh green beans, asparagus, broccoli, peas, peppers, pears, blueberries, cherries, cantaloupe, peaches, plums, and much more. Enjoy!

TRY THIS RECIPE
Arkansas-style Corn Dodgers

Corn dodgers are little balls of fried or baked cornmeal. In earlier days in Arkansas, they were served with bacon and buttermilk. Be sure to have an adult help.

Ingredients:
2 cups yellow cornmeal
1 teaspoon salt
1 tablespoon butter (melted)
2 cups boiling water

Instructions:
1. Preheat the oven to 400°F.
2. Blend the cornmeal and salt in a large bowl.
3. Using a wooden spoon, mix in the melted butter.
4. Slowly mix in boiling water until the dough is moist but still firm enough to shape.
5. Drop heaping spoonfuls of the batter on an ungreased cookie sheet. Shape into mounds (the traditional way) or any shape you want (the fun way).
6. Bake 20 to 25 minutes until crispy and golden brown on the outside. Serve immediately.

Corn dodger

A group of students attend a ceremony at Little Rock Central High School.

SCHOOL DAYS

Arkansas's first public schools opened in the 1840s. Due to a lack of government funding, the state's educational system lagged behind many other states. School systems had little money to maintain schools and buy new textbooks. Beginning in the 1970s, Arkansas made a big push to improve education. To keep kids in school, the general assembly passed a law that prevents school dropouts from getting a driver's license until they're 18 years old. (Enrolled students can get their license at age 16.) The state's graduation rates have improved significantly since then.

Major colleges in Arkansas include the University of Arkansas at Fayetteville, which opened in 1872. Today, it has highly regarded agriculture, architecture, and business programs.

Private colleges in the state include Conway's Hendrix College, which is known for its excellent academics. One of its graduates, Harry Meyer, created a vaccine that prevents German measles. Little Rock's Philander Smith College was founded in 1877 to educate African Americans freed from slavery.

LITERATURE

Arkansas has a rich literary tradition filled with works that draw on the state's landscape and lifestyle. In *Back Yonder* (1932), author Wayman Hogue describes his early life in the Ozarks. Maya Angelou's *I Know Why the Caged Bird Sings* (1969) tells about her life while growing up in the small town of Stamps.

John Gould Fletcher of Little Rock received the Pulitzer Prize for poetry in 1938 for *Selected Poems*. He was the first southern poet to receive the prestigious prize. Ellen Gilchrist lives in Fayetteville and teaches at the University of Arkansas. She won the National Book Award for her short-story collection *Victory Over Japan* (1984). Legal-thriller

MINI-BIO

MAYA ANGELOU: AUTHOR AND ACTIVIST

Maya Angelou (1928–2014) was born in Missouri but moved to Stamps at age three to live with her grandmother. In her first autobiographical book, *I Know Why the Caged Bird Sings* (1969), Angelou described her childhood in Stamps, examining the realities of racism and segregation in the 1930s. In 1993, she wrote the poem "On the Pulse of the Morning," which she read at the inauguration of President Bill Clinton. In addition to writing poetry and best-selling books, she was a spokesperson for peace, justice, and human rights.

? **Want to know more?** Visit www.factsfornow.scholastic.com and enter the keyword **Arkansas**.

To write *A Painted House*, John Grisham drew from his experiences in Arkansas.

writer John Grisham was born in Jonesboro. He spent summers on his grandparents' farm near Black Oak. In addition to best sellers such as *A Time to Kill* (1989) and *The Pelican Brief* (1992), Grisham wrote *A Painted House* (2001), a novel based on his childhood experiences in Arkansas.

Arkansas has been home to many successful children's book writers. Charles Finger's *Tales from Silver Lands* (1924), a collection of folktales, received the Newbery Medal for best children's book of the year. Bette Greene's *Summer of My German Soldier* (1973) tells the story of a young Jewish girl living in Arkansas who befriends an escaped German prisoner of war from World War II, who is supposed to be her enemy. It was made into a film of the same title.

MUSIC

Arkansas has produced many popular musicians. Country-and-western music superstar Johnny Cash was born in Kingsland and grew up in Dyess. Glen Campbell, Conway Twitty, Charlie Rich, Patsy Montana, and Ronnie Dunn are other top country-and-western musicians born in Arkansas. Traditional, fiddle-based music from the Ozarks remains popular with fans of folk music.

MINI-BIO

SONNY BOY WILLIAMSON: HARMONICA-HONKING BLUESMAN

Sonny Boy Williamson (c. 1912–1965) was born Alex Miller on a plantation in Mississippi. In 1949, he moved to West Memphis, Arkansas, where he regularly performed with his musician friends on a local radio station. He recorded extensively during the 1950s and 1960s, making hit records and achieving great success in the United States and abroad. Most experts consider Williamson to be one of the greatest blues harmonica players ever. Among his best-known songs are "Don't Start Me Talkin'," "Nine Below Zero," and "Help Me."

? Want to know more? Visit www.factsfor now.scholastic.com and enter the keyword **Arkansas**.

Arkansas native Johnny Cash was a legendary country music performer.

Although no one knows exactly where blues music began, the Mississippi Delta—the cotton country of southeastern Arkansas and northwestern Mississippi—was a hotbed of blues talent. Arkansas blues greats include Bill Broonzy, Howlin' Wolf, Robert Lockwood, Sonny Boy Williamson, and Son Seals. Cotton Plant native Rosetta Tharpe was the best-known gospel singer in the mid-1900s.

Classical music fans will recognize the work of composer William Grant Still and sopranos Mary Lewis and Barbara Hendricks. Arkansas's location on the busy Mississippi River contributed to the spread of jazz music throughout the state.

SEE IT HERE!

DELTA CULTURAL CENTER

The Delta Cultural Center in Helena features exhibits on the music of Arkansas's Delta region. You can hear recordings of regional blues, gospel, and early rock 'n' roll music. You can also learn about the area's legendary musicians, from Sonny Boy Williamson and Louis Jordan to Johnny Cash and Conway Twitty. A daily blues radio show, *King Biscuit Time*, is broadcast from the center. This radio show, which began broadcasting in 1941, introduced many Americans to southern music.

A steady stream of jazz musicians from New Orleans and Memphis passed through Arkansas. Composer Scott Joplin, bandleader Louis Jordan, singer Al Hibbler, and pianist Art Porter Sr. were all born and raised in Arkansas.

MOUNTAIN CULTURE

Arkansas has a strong crafts and folk art tradition. Arkansas artisans still engage in a wide range of pioneer arts and crafts, including basketry, blacksmithing, broom making, furniture making, needlecrafts, and pottery.

Many of these skills are on display at the Ozark Folk Center in Mountain View. This center was established in 1972 to preserve the culture and history of the Ozark region. Jimmy Driftwood, a popular folksinger and song-writer, helped establish the center.

SPORTS

Because it has no large cities, Arkansas hosts no teams in the major U.S. professional leagues. Fans from around the state cheer for a minor league baseball team, the Arkansas Travelers of Little Rock. College football is an obsession in the state. The University of Arkansas Razorbacks have had great success. Frank Broyles led the Razorbacks football program as coach and athletic director for 49 years. Coaching greats Paul "Bear" Bryant and Barry Switzer were also born and raised in Arkansas.

Basketball is another big sport in Arkansas. The University of Arkansas won the NCAA men's basketball championship in 1994. Hamburg native Scottie Pippen was a key member of the Chicago Bulls in the 1990s. He helped the team win six NBA championships.

The Arkansas Sports Hall of Fame in North Little Rock celebrates the outstanding athletes who were born in or have played in or lived in Arkansas. It honors ath-

Cheerleaders shout as an Arkansas Razorback runs in for a touchdown.

letes such as Baseball Hall of Famers Lou Brock and Dizzy Dean, golfer John Daly, NASCAR driver Mark Martin, and many others.

John Daly tees off at the 1994 British Open.

READ ABOUT

Members of the Arkansas House of Representatives meet in 2013 to discuss tax cuts.

CHAPTER SEVEN

GOVERNMENT

★

GOVERNMENTS HAVE A BIG JOB TO DO. They provide schools, libraries, and fire protection. They maintain parks and make sure that laws are followed. In Arkansas in recent years, the state government has focused on providing its citizens, particularly children, with better health care and improving the quality of public education. Other recent government accomplishments include improving the state's road system and adopting laws that protect the state's environment.

THE ARKANSAS CONSTITUTION

Like many states, Arkansas has had more than one constitution. The first of its five constitutions was written in 1836, when Arkansas became a state. Arkansas adopted a new constitution in 1861, when it seceded from the Union. In 1864, a new constitution was needed to bring Arkansas back into the Union. Another constitution was written in 1868, when the state returned to the Union. The current constitution was adopted in 1874.

Many Arkansans disliked the state government during the Reconstruction period. So the 1874 constitution placed many limits on the government's powers. For example, it lowered the terms of state officials from four years to two years. It also allowed the legislature to meet for only 60 days every two years. The 1874 constitution has been changed many times over the years. For example, governors and senators now serve four-year terms. Most of its provisions, however, are still in force. The constitution establishes the powers and duties of the three branches of the state government: executive, legislative, and judicial.

Because it looks so much like the Capitol in Washington, D.C., the Arkansas capitol appears in many Hollywood films as a stand-in for the U.S. Capitol.

The state capitol in Little Rock

Capital City

This map shows places of interest in Little Rock, Arkansas's capital city.

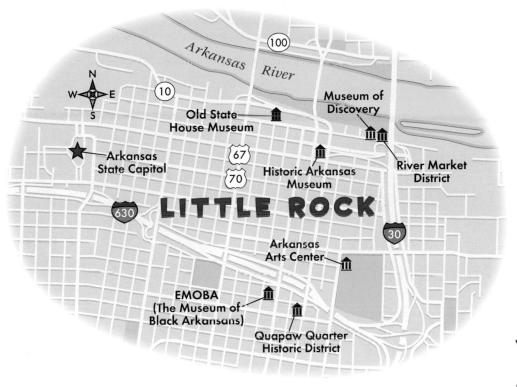

THE EXECUTIVE BRANCH

The governor heads Arkansas's executive branch. Voters elect a governor for a four-year term, and a governor cannot serve more than two terms in a row. The governor's duties include preparing the state budget and appointing members of state departments and commissions. The governor may also suggest new laws to the general assembly. The governor has the power to sign bills into law or veto (reject) them. The legislature, however, can override the veto with a simple majority vote. (In most states, it takes a two-thirds majority to override a governor's veto.)

The governor also oversees the work of more than 150 state agencies that administer state laws and provide

WOW

Arkansas has the oldest capitol west of the Mississippi.

Capitol Facts

Here are some fascinating facts about Arkansas's state capitol:

Exterior height: 213 feet (65 m)
Number of stories high: 4
Length: 440 feet (134 m)
Width: 195 feet (59 m)
Location: 500 Woodlane Avenue, Little Rock
Construction dates: 1899–1915
The capitol was built on the grounds of a state prison. Many prisoners helped in the construction.

Governor Mike Beebe (right) meets with Arkansas state representatives in 2013.

services to residents. These agencies include the Department of Education, the Department of Environmental Quality, and the Motor Vehicle Commission.

Other officials in the executive branch include the lieutenant governor, who takes over if the governor can no longer perform his or her duties, and the secretary of state, who oversees elections. The attorney general represents the state in legal matters, and the treasurer is in charge of state funds.

THE LEGISLATIVE BRANCH

The general assembly's job is to make new laws and change or get rid of old laws. It also recommends changes to the state's constitution. The Arkansas senate has 35 members who serve four-year terms. The Arkansas house of repre-

Representing Arkansas

This list shows the number of elected officials who represent Arkansas, both on the state and national levels.

OFFICE	NUMBER	LENGTH OF TERM
State senators	35	4 years
State representatives	100	2 years
U.S. senators	2	6 years
U.S. representatives	4	2 years
Presidential electors	6	—

sentatives has 100 members who serve two-year terms. Senators may be reelected once, while representatives may be re-elected twice. Because the general assembly meets only every two years, its members also have other

Arkansas State Government

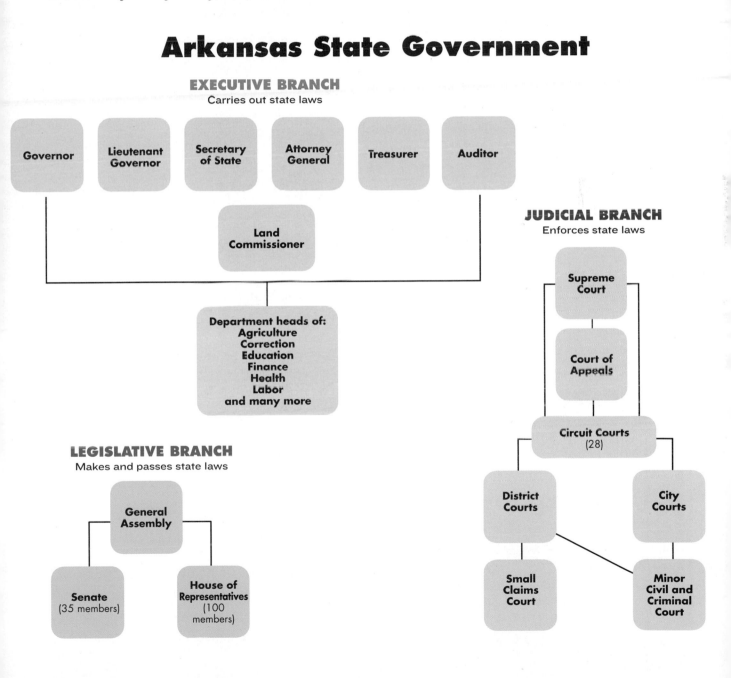

EXECUTIVE BRANCH
Carries out state laws

- Governor
- Lieutenant Governor
- Secretary of State
- Attorney General
- Treasurer
- Auditor

Land Commissioner

Department heads of:
Agriculture
Correction
Education
Finance
Health
Labor
and many more

JUDICIAL BRANCH
Enforces state laws

- Supreme Court
- Court of Appeals
- Circuit Courts (28)
- District Courts
- City Courts
- Small Claims Court
- Minor Civil and Criminal Court

LEGISLATIVE BRANCH
Makes and passes state laws

- General Assembly
- Senate (35 members)
- House of Representatives (100 members)

LOTTIE SHACKELFORD: GROUNDBREAKING POLITICIAN

In 1987, Lottie Shackelford (1941–) became the first woman elected mayor of Little Rock. Before that, she had served on the city's board of directors. Two years after she left office in 1991, President Bill Clinton appointed her to help manage the Overseas Private Investment Corporation (OPIC). Shackelford was the first African American to serve in that role. OPIC is a U.S. government institution that invests money in foreign housing, agriculture, and finance. Shackelford has also worked with the Democratic National Committee, the organization that governs the Democratic Party.

Want to know more? Visit www.factsfornow .scholastic.com and enter the keyword **Arkansas**.

The Pulaski County Courthouse in Little Rock is on the National Register of Historic Places.

Q8 HOW DID CIRCUIT COURTS GET THEIR NAME?

A8 In the old days, judges traveled around a large area, making a circuit (circle), to hold trials in different towns. Today, there are many more judges and courts, so judges don't have to travel.

jobs. Lawyers, ranchers, teachers, and people in many other professions represent their fellow citizens in the general assembly.

THE JUDICIAL BRANCH

Arkansas's courts make up the judicial branch of government. Circuit courts are the major trial courts in the state. Judges on the circuit courts preside over criminal trials and civil cases, such as disputes over property or personal injury. The state has 28 circuit court districts. Voters elect circuit court judges, who serve a six-year term. County and city courts handle minor cases on a local level.

The court of appeals has 12 members who are elected to eight-year terms. If a person thinks a mistake was made in a trial court case, he or she can ask the court of appeals to review the decision. The Arkansas

Arkansas Counties

This map shows the 75 counties in Arkansas. Little Rock, the state capital, is indicated with a star.

Arkansas citizens line up to vote in the 2012 presidential election.

Supreme Court is the highest court in the state. Voters elect its seven justices to eight-year terms. These justices review decisions made by the court of appeals. The supreme court also handles all cases that question whether a state law is valid under the Arkansas constitution.

LOCAL RULE

Arkansas has 75 counties. A county judge serves as the chief executive of each county, overseeing the work of county officials. Voters elect the county judges. Most Arkansas cities are headed by a mayor, and a city council passes local laws.

CITIZEN ACTION

Arkansas gives its citizens the power to propose new laws. This process is called citizens' **initiative**. By collecting enough signatures, Arkansans can place their own proposed law on a ballot. They can then vote for or against laws written by other voters. They can also reject laws passed by the general assembly. Arkansans sometimes use the citizens' initiative process to propose amendments, or changes, to the state constitution. For example, in 1992, a successful citizens' initiative reduced the number of terms that state legislators could serve.

At the local level, citizens in some counties have formed Local Improvements Districts (LIDs). These groups work on projects that improve their communities, such as sprucing up downtown business districts and setting up health clinics. LIDs also have proposed laws to the general assembly.

MINI-BIO

BILL CLINTON: FROM A TOWN CALLED HOPE

William Jefferson Clinton (1946–) was born in Hope and raised in Hot Springs. Even as a child, he knew he wanted to go into politics, so after completing college and law school, he returned to Arkansas to teach law and begin his political career. He was elected governor in 1978 at age 32 and served again as governor from 1983 until 1992. Clinton could discuss any policy issue in detail, and he was elected U.S. president in 1992 and reelected in 1996. As president, he balanced the federal government's budget and reformed the welfare system. He is the only Arkansan ever to serve as U.S. president.

? **Want to know more?** Visit www.factsfornow.scholastic.com and enter the keyword **Arkansas**.

WORD TO KNOW

initiative *a process that allows voters to propose new laws*

State Flag

Arkansas's state flag consists of a white diamond shape with a blue band on a red rectangular field. The diamond shape signifies that Arkansas is the only diamond-producing state. The 25 white stars in the diamond's blue band symbolize that Arkansas was the 25th state to join the Union. Inside the white diamond, the blue star above the word *Arkansas* indicates that Arkansas was a member of the Confederate States during the Civil War. The three stars below *Arkansas* represent the United States, Spain, and France, the three countries that have ruled the region.

State Seal

The Great Seal of Arkansas depicts an angel of mercy at the left and a goddess of liberty on the top. To the right is a sword of justice, and in the center is a bald eagle. In its beak, the eagle holds a scroll with the words *Regnat Populus*, which is Latin for "the people rule." In its talons, the eagle holds an olive branch and a bundle of arrows. A shield in front of the eagle depicts a steamboat, a plow, a beehive, and a sheaf of wheat. These four items symbolize the state's industry and agricultural resources.

98

READ ABOUT

Front desk clerks at
a hotel in Little Rock

CHAPTER EIGHT

ECONOMY

★

FOR MUCH OF ARKANSAS'S HISTORY, MOST PEOPLE WORKED ON FARMS. They worked long days raising cotton, rice, and vegetables. Today, some Arkansans continue to grow rice and cotton, but more work in manufacturing, making items from buses to paper. Arkansans are even more likely to work in offices, hospitals, or schools. And lots of Arkansans work at Walmart, the world's largest corporation.

A cotton farmer checks on his crop.

Arkansas produces almost half of all the rice grown in the United States!

DOWN ON THE FARM

Arkansas's rich topsoil has supported farming for centuries. Today, there are 14.5 million acres (5.9 million ha) of farmland in the state.

Arkansas leads the nation in the production of rice. Introduced in the state in the early 1900s, rice replaced cotton as Arkansas's most valuable crop in the 1960s. The southeastern part of the state provides perfect conditions for growing rice. This region has a warm climate, fertile soil, and good water supplies. Although cotton is no longer king in Arkansas, the state still ranks near the top in cotton production. Arkansas is also a major producer of soybeans and pecans. Other major crops grown by Arkansas farmers are hay, tomatoes, peaches, apples, watermelons, corn, and wheat.

Major Agricultural and Mining Products

This map shows where Arkansas's major agricultural and mining products come from. See a milk carton? That means dairy products are found there.

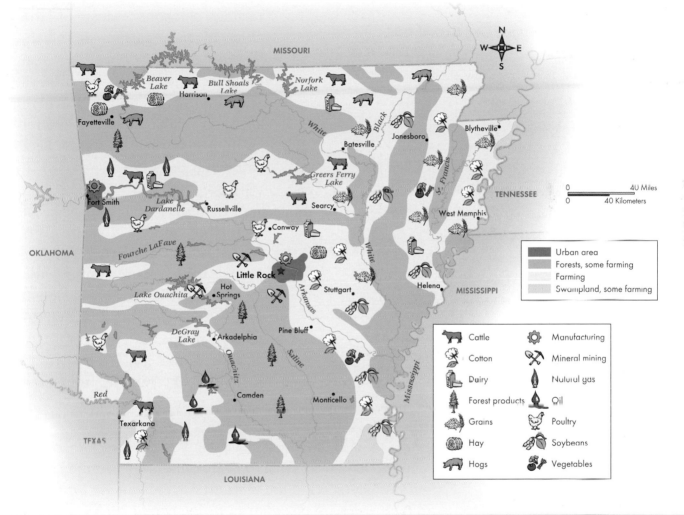

PINK LIKE A TOMATO?

In the 1920s, farmers in southeastern Arkansas noticed something unusual about one type of tomato that they were growing. Instead of being red like most tomatoes, this one had a pinkish color. The pink tomato was soft, juicy, and flavorful. It became popular throughout Arkansas and the rest of the South. In 1987, the General Assembly named the South Arkansas vine ripe pink tomato as the state fruit and the state vegetable. (Tomatoes are technically a fruit, but they're eaten like a vegetable.) A Pink Tomato Festival is held each year in Warren. It features a parade, a lunch with all the dishes made with tomatoes, and a tomato-eating contest.

WINTHROP ROCKEFELLER: ATTRACTING BUSINESS

Winthrop Rockefeller (1912–1973) was born into a wealthy New York family, but he always longed for adventure. After visiting a friend in Arkansas, he moved there in 1953 and established a cattle business on his farm west of Little Rock. He eventually entered politics and served as governor from 1967 to 1971. As governor, he helped modernize the state by convincing big businesses to build factories in Arkansas. Today, his Winthrop Rockefeller Foundation provides money for educational, public health, and social justice projects throughout Arkansas.

 Want to know more? Visit www.factsfornow.scholastic.com and enter the keyword **Arkansas**.

LIVESTOCK AND FISH

Poultry is the state's most important type of livestock. Arkansas ranks second in the country in raising chickens. Most of the chickens are raised in northwestern Arkansas. The state also ranks second in raising turkeys and 10th in producing eggs. There are many dairy farms in central and northwestern Arkansas. Beef cattle and hogs are also raised in the state.

Arkansas is the birthplace of catfish farming. Two fish farms started selling catfish in the 1950s. Today, Arkansas ranks among the top states in the country in catfish production. The catfish are raised in large ponds, ranging from 10 to 20 acres (4 to 8 ha). They eat food pellets made mostly from soybeans, grains, and vitamins.

MADE IN ARKANSAS

What do Arkansans make? They produce everything from automobile parts to the chicken fingers you eat for lunch to the cardboard box your morning cereal comes in.

In the 1960s, the state, particularly under Governor Winthrop Rockefeller, began attracting manufacturing companies. Today, manufacturers employ about 14 percent of the state's workforce. Many of the products manufactured in Arkansas are made with raw materials produced in the state. While the number of manufactur-

These workers are manufacturing hardwood lumber in Des Arc.

ing jobs has decreased overall in the state since 2000, some sectors of the state's manufacturing economy continue to be strong.

The state's most important manufacturing segment is food processing. It accounts for about 25 percent of the state's industrial employment. Workers in food processing plants operate the equipment that turns farm produce into food products. Major food products that are processed in Arkansas include poultry products, rice, canned vegetables, meats, milk, cottonseed oil, and animal feed. Tyson Foods, based in Springdale, is the world's largest poultry processor. Riceland Foods, based in Stuttgart, is the world's largest rice packager and exporter.

The state's second-largest industry is the manufacturing of machinery and equipment, such as engines and turbines. The manufacture of metals is another major industry in Arkansas.

Timber goods remain important in Arkansas, although the wood products industry in the state has been on the decline since about 2008. As the U.S. economy slumped during the worldwide financial crisis, the demand for lumber in the housing industry fell off because fewer houses were being built. The reduced demand for wood resulted in the loss of thousands of timber industry jobs.

Biofuel manufacturing is a relatively new and growing industry in the state. Biofuels are energy sources made from plants. For example, corn is used to make ethanol, and

THINK ABOUT IT!

Biofuels

PRO

One way to make the United States less dependent on oil supplies from other countries is to make biofuels. Bob Dineen, director of the Renewable Fuels Association, has stated, "Biofuels like ethanol are the only tool readily available that can begin to address the challenges of energy security and environmental protection." Supporters of biofuel production point out that it provides farmers with a new market for their crops and creates new jobs in refineries. Biofuels also create less air pollution than gasoline or diesel fuel. Scientists are developing crops that can be planted in less fertile soil. These new fuel crops will allow farmers to use their fertile fields to grow enough food crops.

CON

Biofuel production leads to more farmland being used to grow crops for fuel instead of food. Food prices increase because fewer food crops are grown. Opponents of biofuel production also argue that biofuels are not an efficient source of fuel. Some studies have shown that the amount of energy needed to make a gallon of ethanol is greater than the amount of energy that gallon of ethanol produces. One researcher, Cornell University ecology professor David Pimentel, has observed, "The United States desperately needs a liquid fuel replacement for oil in the near future, but producing ethanol or biodiesel from plant[s] [uses] more energy … than you get … from [burning] these products." The best way to make the United States less dependent on foreign oil, some people say, is to take steps to conserve fuel.

soybeans are used to make bio-diesel. Ethanol and biodiesel can be used as fuel for cars, trains, and other machines. Arkansas's first biodiesel plant opened in 2005. Today, the state has four plants.

MINING

Arkansas has a wealth of minerals and other underground natural resources. The oil and natural gas industry provides thousands of jobs, with the average worker earning about twice the average pay of all industries in Arkansas.

Top Products

Agriculture crops	Rice, soybeans, cotton, hay, wheat, corn, sorghum, grapes, peaches, tomatoes, apples, watermelons
Agriculture livestock	Chickens, cattle, calves, chicken eggs, turkeys, catfish, hogs
Manufacturing	Food products; forestry products, including manufactured paper products; chemicals; electrical products; metal products; car parts; plastic and rubber products
Mining	Natural gas, oil, bromine, bauxite, crushed stone, clay, coal, gypsum, limestone

A worker inspects connections while installing a gas pipeline in southern Arkansas.

FAQ

Q: WHAT IS NATURAL GAS?
A: Natural gas is a colorless gas that is found underneath the earth's surface. It burns easily and is used for heating, cooking, and other purposes.

Arkansas is the nation's number-one producer of bauxite and bromine. Bauxite is the ore refined into aluminum, a lightweight metal. Bauxite mines are located in the northern part of the West Gulf Coastal Plain. Bromine is a reddish liquid that is used in fire retardants, insect sprays, disinfectants, and other chemicals. Bromine is found in the West Gulf Coastal Plain. It is removed from **brines** that are pumped up from beneath the earth's surface. Other key earth materials found in Arkansas include titanium, coal, diamonds, limestone, soapstone, crushed stone, cement, sand, and gravel.

WORD TO KNOW

brines *liquids that have a high salt content*

MINI-BIO

WILLIAM DILLARD: DEPARTMENT STORE MOGUL

With $8,000 he borrowed from his father, Little Rock native William T. Dillard (1914–2002) opened up his first retail store, in Nashville, Arkansas, in 1938. He eventually opened more stores in Texas and throughout the southern United States. Recognizing the growing popularity of suburban shopping malls, Dillard opened stores in mall locations during the 1960s and 1970s. By the end of the century, Dillard's, based in Little Rock, was the third-largest department store chain in America.

? Want to know more? Visit www.factsfornow .scholastic.com and enter the keyword **Arkansas**.

BIG BUSINESS

As in most other states, service businesses make up a large portion of the state's economy. Service businesses include everything from doctors and lawyers to hotels and barbershops. Schools, military bases, banks, and real estate services are also important to the state's economy. Telephone, Internet, gas, and electric companies are part of the service sector as well.

Many major corporations got their start in Arkansas, including Tyson Foods and Walmart, two of the largest employers in the state. Walmart is the company most associated with Arkansas. Brothers Sam and Bud Walton

What Do Arkansans Do?

This color-coded chart shows what industries Arkansans work in.

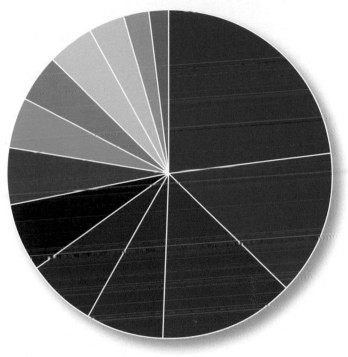

23.3%	Educational services, and health care and social assistance 292,178
14.2%	Manufacturing 178,206
13.3%	Retail trade 167,010
7.6%	Arts, entertainment, and recreation, and accommodation and food services 95,550
7.0%	Construction 87,424
6.8%	Professional, scientific, and management, and administrative and waste management services 85,256
5.5%	Transportation and warehousing, and utilities 69,146
5.0%	Finance and insurance, and real estate and rental and leasing 62,565
4.8%	Other services, except public administration 60,121
4.7%	Public administration 59,294
3.4%	Agriculture, forestry, fishing and hunting, and mining 42,061
2.7%	Wholesale trade 33,254
1.7%	Information 21,004

Source: U.S. Census Bureau, 2010 census

opened their first Walmart store in Rogers in 1962. By 2013, their company was the world's largest retail store chain, with more than 11,000 stores and two million employees worldwide. The stores generate hundreds of billions of dollars in sales each year. Walmart's headquarters is located in Bentonville, and the company has spurred the growth of northwest Arkansas. It has attracted many businesses to the region, especially those that make products for Walmart to sell.

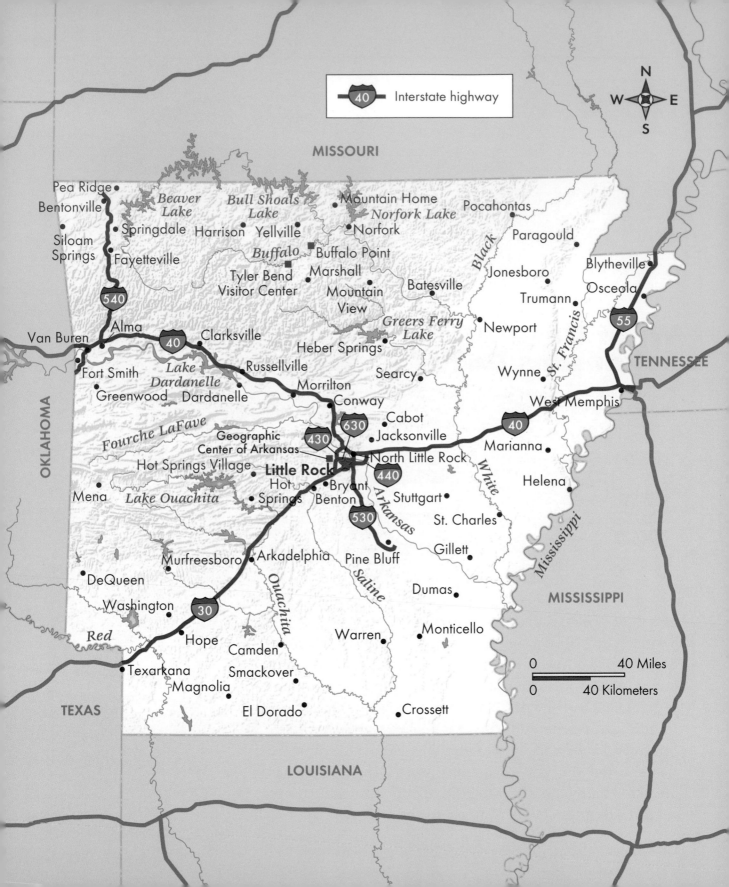

N
W ◆ E
S

40 Interstate highway

MISSOURI

Pea Ridge
Bentonville
Siloam Springs
Beaver Lake
Springdale
Bull Shoals Lake
Harrison Yellville
Mountain Home
Norfork Lake
Norfork
Pocahontas
Paragould
Fayetteville
Buffalo Buffalo Point
Batesville
Blytheville
Osceola
Tyler Bend Visitor Center
Marshall
Jonesboro
Trumann
540
Mountain View
Greers Ferry Lake
Newport
Van Buren
Alma
Clarksville
Heber Springs
Searcy
Wynne
West Memphis
40
Fort Smith
Russellville
Lake Dardanelle
Conway
Cabot
Jacksonville
Marianna
TENNESSEE
55
Greenwood
Dardanelle
Morrilton
630
North Little Rock
Helena
Fourche LaFave
430
Geographic Center of Arkansas
Hot Springs Village
Little Rock
Stuttgart
440
Mena
Lake Ouachita
Hot Springs
Bryant
Benton
Arkansas
St. Charles
White
530
Gillett
Murfreesboro
Arkadelphia
Pine Bluff
Dumas
Saline
Ouachita
MISSISSIPPI
DeQueen
Warren
Monticello
Washington
30
Mississippi
Red
Hope
Camden
Crossett
Texarkana
Smackover
Magnolia
El Dorado

0   40 Miles
0   40 Kilometers

OKLAHOMA

TEXAS

LOUISIANA

St. Francis

Black

TRAVEL GUIDE

★

COZY MOUNTAINS. Dense forests. Remote waterways. Get out there and enjoy Arkansas's natural beauty! Hike up a mountain. Explore a cave. Go white-water rafting down a wild river. Take a dip in a mineral spring. And don't forget the cities! Visit a museum in Little Rock. Check out the fort in Fort Smith. From Alma to Yellville, Arkansas's small cities also have lots to offer.

← Follow along with this travel map. We'll start in Jonesboro, go clockwise around the state, and end in the center at North Little Rock.

NORTHEAST

THINGS TO DO: Imagine you're a pioneer farmer, check out a NASCAR driver's museum, and go trout fishing atop Crowley's Ridge.

Jonesboro

★ **Crowley's Ridge State Park:** Enjoy camping, hiking, swimming, picnicking, and fishing at this park on top of Crowley's Ridge. You can also rent a water bike for a spin around the lake.

Batesville

★ **Mark Martin Museum:** If you're a NASCAR fan, don't miss this museum dedicated to race-car driver Mark Martin. It follows Martin's path from local dirt tracks to the big time and showcases some of his past race cars, trophies, and racing mementos.

Pocahontas

★ **Living Farm Museum:** See demonstrations of old farm equipment, such as antique tractors, horse-drawn plows, threshers, and balers.

SOUTHEAST

THINGS TO DO: Listen to the blues, look for turtles and salamanders, and learn how meals were cooked in the 19th century.

Pine Bluff

★ **Delta Rivers Nature Center:** Built like an old Delta hunting lodge, the center shows the importance of streams and wetlands to the Delta region. The center also features live wildlife and a 20,000-gallon (76,000 l) aquarium.

Helena

★ **King Biscuit Blues Festival:** Blues music was born in the Delta region of Arkansas and Mississippi. This is the place to be every October if you want to hear the region's best blues musicians.

Musicians at the King Biscuit Blues Festival

Gillett

★ **Arkansas Post Museum:** Here you can see how settlers lived in 19th-century Arkansas. In the kitchen building, learn how meals were cooked on an open fireplace. The museum also has a great toy collection from the 1920s and 1930s.

St. Charles

★ **White River National Wildlife Refuge:** Stop at the visitors' center to learn about the area's plants and wildlife, and then ask a ranger to recommend a hike. You might spot salamanders, turtles, swamp rabbits, or even a fox.

SOUTHWEST
THINGS TO DO: Look for arrowheads, ride the Arkansas Twister roller coaster, and enter a watermelon seed–spitting competition.

Murfreesboro

★ **Ka-Do-Ha Indian Village:** Mound Builders once lived on this site, and today ancient tools, pottery, weapons, and jewelry are on display. As you walk around the village, keep an eye out for arrowheads on the ground.

THE NATURAL STATE
In 1995, Arkansas's legislature changed the state's official nickname to the Natural State. The law said that the new name would call attention to the state's "unsurpassed scenery, clear lakes, free-flowing streams, magnificent rivers, meandering bayous, delta bottomlands, forested mountains, and abundant fish and wildlife."

Hot Springs

★ **Hot Springs National Park:** People have been traveling to Hot Springs to enjoy the mineral springs for more than two centuries. You can tour one of the historic bathhouses or take a traditional mineral bath.

Visitors at Hot Springs National Park

A roller coaster at Magic Springs

★ **Magic Springs & Crystal Falls:** Take a splash in the water park or enjoy rides at the theme park. If you dare, hop aboard one of the park's several roller coasters. Consider yourself warned about the legendary Arkansas Twister!

★ **Bill Clinton sites:** As you explore Hot Springs, you can see President Clinton's boyhood home, high school, church, and hangouts all over town.

Washington

★ **Historic Washington State Park:** Travel back in time to an 1850s frontier boomtown. Stroll along plank-board sidewalks, tour the historic buildings, and get a feel for what Washington was like when Davy Crockett, Sam Houston, and other frontiersmen passed through the town.

Texarkana

★ **Discovery Place:** This museum is filled with hands-on experiments involving science, history, and human perception.

Smackover

★ **Arkansas Museum of Natural Resources:** Learn all about the oil and brine industries, from how oil was created to how it is brought to the earth's surface. The museum even features full-size oil derricks (towers over the drilling holes). An added attraction is the restored 1920s circus wagon of the "Goat Woman." She was a circus performer who settled in Smackover during its boom days and started raising goats.

Hope

★ **Watermelon Festival:** Every August, Hope hosts a watermelon festival. It features a watermelon-eating contest, a seed-spitting contest, hillbilly horseshoes, and other fun activities. If you enter the watermelon-eating contest, don't fill up on corn dogs, pork rinds, or other local favorites beforehand.

NORTHWEST

THINGS TO DO: Explore a giant cave, ride an old trolley, hear some toe-tapping music, and see where Walmart got its start.

Fort Smith

★ **Fort Smith Trolley Museum:** Ride a fully restored 1926 electric trolley from the museum to the Fort Smith Historic Site. In the museum, you can examine old railroad cars, engines, and Fort Smith buses.

★ **Fort Smith National Historic Site:** While exploring the remains of the original 1817 fort, you'll see the barracks that soldiers lived in that later became the courthouse for Isaac Parker, the "Hanging Judge."

Springdale

★ **Arkansas and Missouri Railroad:** Hop aboard this restored 1900s passenger train for a 134-mile (216 km) round-trip through the region.

Morrilton

★ **Museum of Automobiles:** Check out cars dating from 1904 to the late 1960s. Former governor Winthrop Rockefeller started the museum, and some of the cars are from his collection.

★ **Cedar Falls:** Hike the Cedar Falls Trail at Petit Jean State Park to reach the falls. Water tumbles 95 feet (29 m) from the top.

OZARK FIDDLE MAKER

Violet Hensley is a fiddle maker and traditional musician. She learned to make fiddles from her father. Using hand tools and traditional methods, she has made more than 70 fiddles in her Yellville home. She uses many different kinds of wood from Arkansas trees. Her fiddles are highly prized for their quality. Hensley and her family have made three albums featuring traditional Ozark fiddle music. The Arkansas Arts Council named her an Arkansas Living Treasure in 2004.

Mountain View

★ **Ozark Folk Center State Park:** This living museum helps preserve the music and ways of the Ozarks. See craftspeople make furniture, quilts, wood carvings, tintype photos, and other crafts using traditional methods. Attend a concert to hear traditional Ozarks music.

★ **Blanchard Springs Caverns:** Take a tour of one of the country's best limestone cave systems. One of the caves is larger than three football fields!

Buffalo Point/Tyler Bend

★ **Buffalo National River:** Enjoy hiking, canoeing, white-water rafting, horseback riding, and all sorts of other outdoor activities. Keep an eye out for elk!

Pea Ridge

★ **Pea Ridge National Military Park:** Take the self-guided tour that shows how the largest Civil War battle in Arkansas was fought.

Fayetteville

★ **Arkansas Air & Military Museum:** Check out all the vintage aircraft, including biplanes, helicopters, and an early 20th-century racing plane that can still fly.

Bentonville

★ **The Walmart Museum:** You can see the Waltons' original tiny office and find out how this small Arkansas store grew into the world's largest corporation.

Norfolk

★ **Wolf House:** See furniture and other items from a log cabin built in the 1810s. It's believed to be the oldest log cabin in Arkansas.

SEE IT HERE!

THE SHOE TREES OF CARROLL COUNTY

Along Highway 187 outside of Beaver, you'll see trees with shoes hanging from their branches. Thousands of shoes, boots, and even roller skates hung from the branches of the original shoe tree. After a storm destroyed the towering white oak, people started using other nearby trees to keep the tradition going. You can join in the fun by flinging your footwear on one of the trees already wearing shoes. (Don't use any tree on private property.)

CENTRAL ARKANSAS

THINGS TO DO: Learn more about the Little Rock Nine, read presidential documents, and experiment with robots.

Little Rock

★ **Old State House Museum:** Check out the exhibits to learn everything you need to know about Arkansas history.

★ **Historic Arkansas Museum:** Here you can learn about the lives of enslaved families in the 1850s.

★ **Little Rock Central High School National Historic Site:** Central High School is still operating. After you take a look at the outside of the building, head across the street to the visitors' center. The exhibit titled "All the World Is Watching Us: Little Rock and the 1957 Crisis" provides details of the desegregation standoff at the school.

Little Rock Central High School

FAQ

Q8 HOW DID LITTLE ROCK GET ITS NAME?

A8 Early French explorers named the spot La Petite Roche ("little rock" in French) because of a little rock on the bank of the Arkansas River.

★ **Museum of Discovery:** Get ready to have fun—science fun! Take part in experiments involving electricity, robots, computers, and human anatomy.

★ **Arkansas Arts Center:** See works by Vincent van Gogh, Georgia O'Keeffe, and Rembrandt at this world-class art museum.

★ **Clinton Presidential Center:** The center's library holds official papers and artifacts from Bill Clinton's presidency.

North Little Rock

★ **Arkansas Inland Maritime Museum:** See the USS *Razorback*, a submarine that served in World War II and the Vietnam War. (It's named after the razorback whale, not the razorback hog.) You can also see other types of boats and learn about the impact Arkansas's many waterways have had on the state.

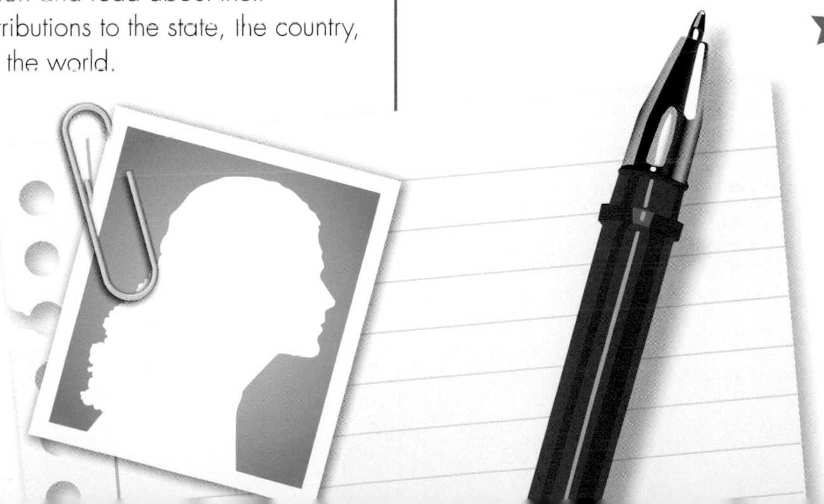

WRITING PROJECTS

Write a Memoir, Journal, or Editorial for Your School Newspaper!

Picture Yourself . . .

★ Building a grass house with the Caddo people. What kinds of materials would you need, and where could you gather these materials? Describe how you and the other members of your community build the house.

   SEE: Chapter Two, pages 28–29.

★ As one of the Little Rock Nine. Describe what you see, hear, and feel as you walk through an angry crowd on the first day of school. Explain why you chose to go to school that day, even though you knew it might be dangerous.

   SEE: Chapter Five, pages 63–67.

Create an Election Brochure or Web Site!

Run for office! Throughout this book, you've read about some of the issues that concern Arkansas today. As a candidate for governor of Arkansas, create a campaign brochure or Web site.

★ Explain how you meet the qualifications to be governor of Arkansas.

★ Talk about the three or four major issues you'll focus on if you're elected.

★ Remember, you'll be responsible for Arkansas's budget. How would you spend the taxpayers' money?

   SEE: Chapter Seven, pages 89–91.

Create an interview script with a famous person from Arkansas!

★ Research various famous Arkansans, such as Daisy Bates, Bill Clinton, Johnny Cash, Maya Angelou, Paul "Bear" Bryant, and many others.

★ Based on your research, pick one person you would most like to talk with.

★ Write a script of the interview. What questions would you ask? How would this famous person answer? Create a question-and-answer format. You may want to supplement this writing project with a voice-recording dramatization of the interview.

   SEE: Chapters Five, Six, and Seven, pages 66, 81, 82, 84, 95, and the Biographical Dictionary, pages 133–137.

ART PROJECTS

Create a PowerPoint Presentation or Visitors' Guide

Welcome to Arkansas!

Arkansas is a great place to visit and to live! From its natural beauty to its historical sites, there's plenty to see and do. In your PowerPoint presentation or brochure, highlight 10 to 15 of Arkansas's fascinating landmarks. Be sure to include:

★ a map of the state showing where these sites are located

★ photos, illustrations, Web links, natural history facts, geographic stats, climate and weather, plants and wildlife, and recent discoveries

SEE: Chapter Nine, pages 108–115, and Fast Facts, pages 126–127.

Illustrate the Lyrics to the Arkansas State Songs

("Arkansas [You Run Deep in Me]" or "Oh, Arkansas")

Use markers, paints, photos, collages, colored pencils, or computer graphics to illustrate the lyrics to one of the state songs. Turn your illustrations into a picture book, or scan them into PowerPoint and add music.

SEE: The lyrics to "Arkansas (You Run Deep in Me)" or "Oh, Arkansas" on page 128.

Research Arkansas's State Quarter

From 1999 to 2008, the U.S. Mint introduced new quarters commemorating each of the 50 states in the order that they were admitted to the Union. Each state's quarter features a unique design on its reverse, or back.

★ Research the significance of the image. Who designed the quarter? Who chose the final design?

★ Design your own Arkansas quarter. What images would you choose for the reverse?

★ Make a poster showing the Arkansas quarter and label each image.

GO TO: www.factsfornow.scholastic.com. Enter the keyword **Arkansas** and look for the link to the Arkansas quarter.

SCIENCE, TECHNOLOGY, ENGINEERING, & MATH PROJECTS

Graph Population Statistics!

★ Compare population statistics (such as ethnic background, birth, death, and literacy rates) in Arkansas counties or major cities.

★ In your graph or chart, look at population density and write sentences describing what the population statistics show; graph one set of population statistics and write a paragraph explaining what the graphs reveal.

SEE: Chapter Six, pages 72–77.

Create a Weather Map of Arkansas!

Use your knowledge of Arkansas's geography to research and identify conditions that result in specific weather events. What is it about the geography of Arkansas that makes it vulnerable to tornadoes? Create a weather map or poster that shows the weather patterns over the state. Include a caption explaining the technology used to measure weather phenomena and provide data.

SEE: Chapter One, pages 17.

Red-cockaded woodpecker

Track Endangered Species

Using your knowledge of Arkansas's wildlife, research which animals and plants are endangered or threatened.

★ Find out what the state is doing to protect these species.

★ Chart known populations of the animals and plants, and report on changes in certain geographic areas.

SEE: Chapter One, page 20.

PRIMARY VS. SECONDARY SOURCES

What's the Diff?

Your teacher may require at least one or two primary sources and one or two secondary sources for your assignment. So, what's the difference between the two?

★ **Primary sources are original.** You are reading the actual words of someone's diary, journal, letter, autobiography, or interview. Primary sources can also be photographs, maps, prints, cartoons, news/film footage, posters, first-person newspaper articles, drawings, musical scores, and recordings. By the way, when you conduct a survey, interview someone, shoot a video, or take photographs to include in a project, you are creating primary sources!

★ **Secondary sources are what you find in encyclopedias, textbooks, articles, biographies, and almanacs.** These are written by a person or group of people who tell about something that happened to someone else. Secondary sources also recount what another person said or did. This book is an example of a secondary source.

Now that you know what primary sources are—where can you find them?

★ **Your school or local library:** Check the library catalog for collections of original writings, government documents, musical scores, and so on. Some of this material may be stored on microfilm.

★ **Historical societies:** These organizations keep historical documents, photographs, and other materials. Staff members can help you find what you are looking for. History museums are also great places to see primary sources firsthand.

★ **The Internet:** There are lots of sites that have primary sources you can download and use in a project or assignment.

TIMELINE

★ ★ ★

U.S. Events | 10,000 BCE | **Arkansas Events**

c. 10,000 BCE
The first humans arrive in what is now Arkansas.

100 CE

c. 650 CE
The Plum Bayou culture thrives.

800
The Mississippian culture develops.

1000

c. 1000
The Caddo culture emerges in southwestern Arkansas.

1400

1492
Christopher Columbus and his crew sight land in the Caribbean Sea.

1500

1541
Spanish explorer Hernando de Soto arrives in what is now Arkansas.

1565
Spanish admiral Pedro Menéndez de Avilés founds St. Augustine, Florida, the oldest continuously occupied European settlement in the continental United States.

1600

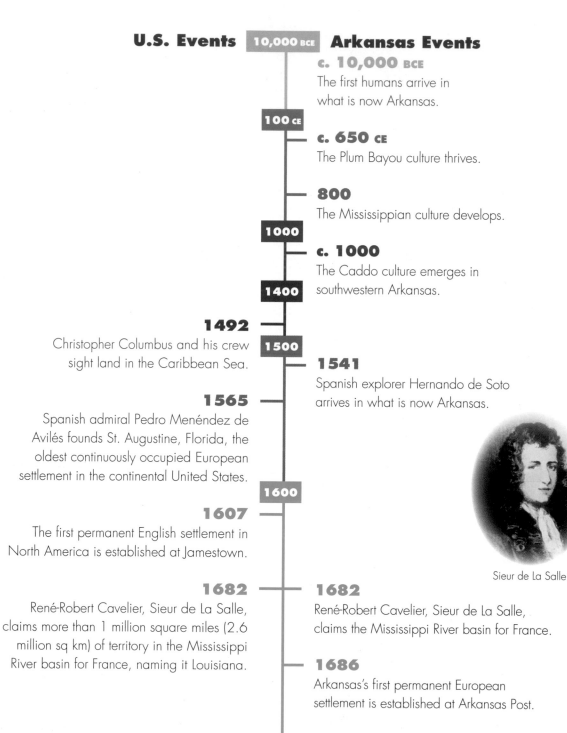

Sieur de La Salle

1607
The first permanent English settlement in North America is established at Jamestown.

1682
René-Robert Cavelier, Sieur de La Salle, claims more than 1 million square miles (2.6 million sq km) of territory in the Mississippi River basin for France, naming it Louisiana.

1682
René-Robert Cavelier, Sieur de La Salle, claims the Mississippi River basin for France.

1686
Arkansas's first permanent European settlement is established at Arkansas Post.

U.S. Events 〔1700〕 Arkansas Events

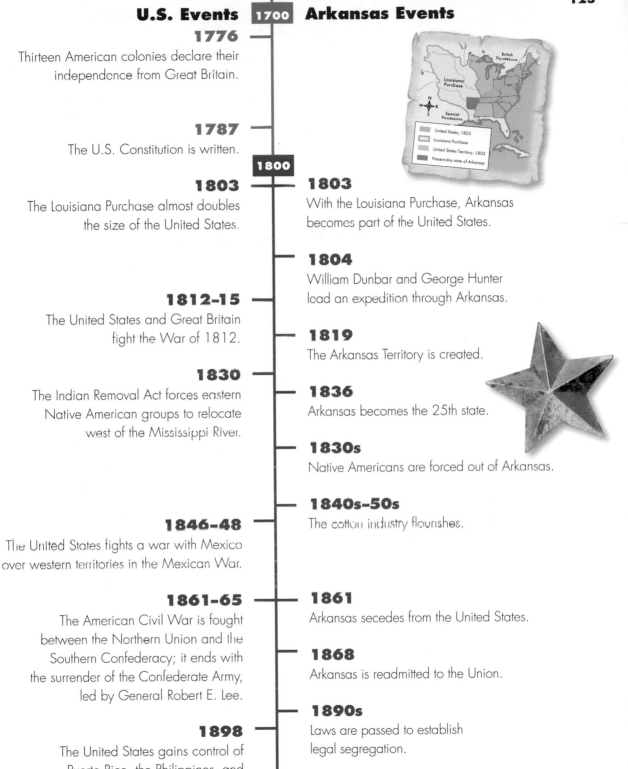

U.S. Events

1776
Thirteen American colonies declare their independence from Great Britain.

1787
The U.S. Constitution is written.

〔1800〕

1803
The Louisiana Purchase almost doubles the size of the United States.

1812-15
The United States and Great Britain fight the War of 1812.

1830
The Indian Removal Act forces eastern Native American groups to relocate west of the Mississippi River.

1846-48
The United States fights a war with Mexico over western territories in the Mexican War.

1861-65
The American Civil War is fought between the Northern Union and the Southern Confederacy; it ends with the surrender of the Confederate Army, led by General Robert E. Lee.

1898
The United States gains control of Puerto Rico, the Philippines, and Guam after defeating Spain in the Spanish-American War.

Arkansas Events

1803
With the Louisiana Purchase, Arkansas becomes part of the United States.

1804
William Dunbar and George Hunter lead an expedition through Arkansas.

1819
The Arkansas Territory is created.

1836
Arkansas becomes the 25th state.

1830s
Native Americans are forced out of Arkansas.

1840s-50s
The cotton industry flourishes.

1861
Arkansas secedes from the United States.

1868
Arkansas is readmitted to the Union.

1890s
Laws are passed to establish legal segregation.

U.S. Events | 1900 | Arkansas Events

1917-18
The United States engages in World War I.

1919
Hundreds of African Americans are killed in Phillips County.

1920
The Nineteenth Amendment to the U.S. Constitution grants women the right to vote.

1927
A flood devastates Arkansas.

1929
The stock market crashes, plunging the United States more deeply into the Great Depression.

1930
A drought strikes Arkansas.

1932
Hattie Wyatt Caraway becomes the first woman elected to the U.S. Senate.

1941-45
The United States engages in World War II.

1950-53
The United States engages in the Korean War.

The Little Rock Nine

1954
The U.S. Supreme Court prohibits segregation of public schools in the *Brown v. Board of Education* ruling.

1957
Violence erupts when Little Rock tries to desegregate its schools.

1962
Walmart is founded.

1964-73
The United States engages in the Vietnam War.

1991
The United States and other nations engage in the brief Persian Gulf War against Iraq.

| 2000 |

1992
Arkansas governor Bill Clinton is elected president.

President Bill Clinton

2001
Terrorists hijack four U.S. aircraft and crash them into the World Trade Center in New York City, the Pentagon in Arlington, Virginia, and a Pennsylvania field, killing thousands.

2002
Arkansas-based Walmart becomes the world's largest corporation.

2003
The United States and coalition forces invade Iraq.

2010
Flash floods kill 20 people at Albert Pike Recreation Area.

GLOSSARY

★ ★ ★

alluvial plain an area that is created when sand, soil, and rocks are carried by water and dropped in a certain place

archaeologists people who study the remains of past human societies

artifacts items created by humans, usually for a practical purpose

bayou a stream that runs slowly through a swamp and leads to or from a river

brines liquids that have a high salt content

ceded gave up or granted

civil rights basic human rights that all citizens in a society are entitled to, such as the right to vote

colony a community settled in a new land but with ties to another government

constitution a written document that contains all the governing principles of a state or country

discrimination unequal treatment based on race, gender, religion, or other factors

endangered in danger of becoming extinct throughout all or part of a range

erosion the gradual wearing away of rock or soil by physical breakdown, chemical solution, or water

fortified strengthened by forts or other protective measures

immunity natural protection against disease

initiative a process that allows voters to propose new laws

integrate to bring together all members of society

levees human-made wall-like embankments, often made of earth, built along a river to control flooding

martyr a person who dies for his or her beliefs

missionary a person who tries to convert others to a religion

secede to withdraw from a group or organization

sediment material eroded from rocks and deposited elsewhere by wind, water, or glaciers

segregation separation from others, according to race, class, ethnic group, religion, or other factors

sit-ins acts of protest that involve sitting in seats or on the floor of an establishment and refusing to leave

stalactites columns or pillars formed on the ceiling of a cave from dripping groundwater

stalagmites columns or pillars formed on the floor of a cave from dripping groundwater

stocks shares in the ownership of a company

threatened likely to become endangered in the foreseeable future

FAST FACTS

★ ★ ★

State Symbols

Statehood date	June 15, 1836, the 25th state
Origin of state name	From the Sioux word *Akansa* meaning "people of the south wind"
State capital	Little Rock
State nickname	The Natural State
State motto	*Regnat Populus* ("The People Rule")
State bird	Mockingbird
State flower	Apple blossom
State mineral	Quartz crystal
State gem	Diamond
State fruit and vegetable	South Arkansas vine ripe pink tomato
State mammal	White-tailed deer
State insect	Honeybee
State songs	"Arkansas (You Run Deep in Me)" and "Oh, Arkansas" (See lyrics on page 128)
State tree	Pine
State fair	Late September–early October at Little Rock

State seal

Geography

Total area; rank	53,178 square miles (137,732 sq km); 29th
Land; rank	52,030 square miles (134,758 sq km); 27th
Water; rank	1,149 square miles (2,976 sq km); 31st
Inland water; rank	1,149 square miles (2,976 sq km); 19th
Geographic center	Pulaski County, about 12 miles (19 km) northwest of Little Rock
Latitude	33° N to 36°30' N
Longitude	89°41' W to 94°42' W
Highest point	Magazine Mountain, 2,753 feet (839 m) in Logan County
Lowest point	55 feet (17 m), where the Ouachita River flows from Arkansas into Louisiana
Largest city	Little Rock
Longest river	Mississippi
Number of counties	75

Population

Population; rank (2010 census)	2,915,918; 32nd
Density (2010 census)	56 persons per square mile (22 per sq km)
Population distribution (2010 census)	56% urban, 44% rural
Ethnic distribution (2010 census)	White persons: 74.5%
	Black persons: 15.3%
	Persons of Hispanic or Latino origin: 6.4%
	Persons reporting two or more races: 1.6%
	Asian persons: 1.2%
	American Indian and Alaska Native persons: 0.7%
	Native Hawaiian and other Pacific Islanders: 0.2%
	Persons of some other race: 0.1%

Weather

Record high temperature	120°F (49°C) at Ozark on August 10, 1936
Record low temperature	−29°F (−34°C) at Benton County on February 13, 1905
Average July temperature, Little Rock	83°F (28°C)
Average January temperature, Little Rock	41°F (5°C)
Average yearly precipitation, Little Rock	51 inches (130 cm)

State flag

STATE SONG

 ★ ★ ★

Two songs were named official state songs in 1987 by the state legislature: "Arkansas (You Run Deep in Me)," by Wayland Holyfield, and "Oh, Arkansas," by Terry Rose and Gary Klaff.

"Arkansas (You Run Deep in Me)"

October morning in the Ozark Mountains,
Hills a blazing like that sun in the sky.
I fell in love there and the fire's still burning
A flame that never will die.

Chorus:
Oh, I may wander, but when I do
I will never be far from you.
You're in my blood and I know you'll always be.
Arkansas, you run deep in me.

"Oh, Arkansas"

It's the spirit of the mountains and the spirit
  of the Delta
It's the spirit of the Capitol dome.
It's the spirit of the river and the spirit of the
  lakes,
It's the spirit that's in each and every home.
It's the spirit of the people and the spirit
  of the land,
It's the spirit of tomorrow and today.

Chorus:
Oh Arkansas, Oh Arkansas, Arkansas U.S.A.
It's the spirit of friendship, it's the spirit of hope
It's the Razorbacks every game they play.
Oh Arkansas, Oh Arkansas, Arkansas U.S.A.

NATURAL AREAS AND HISTORIC SITES

★ ★ ★

National Park
Hot Springs National Park protects 47 hot springs and their watershed. It includes eight different natural bathhouses.

National Memorial
The *Arkansas Post National Memorial* features a museum that details the city's importance during the early days of European settlement of Arkansas.

National Military Park
Pea Ridge National Military Park commemorates the March 1862 Civil War battle. This park is one of the best preserved battlefields in the nation.

National River
Arkansas has one national river meandering within its borders. The *Buffalo National River* is a 135-mile (217 km) stretch of unpolluted, free-flowing river. It is popular with canoeists and kayakers.

National Historic Sites
The *Little Rock Central High School National Historic Site* commemorates the struggle to end segregation in public schools.

The *Fort Smith National Historic Site* offers visitors a chance to walk part of the Trail of Tears and explore old military buildings from the active days of Fort Smith.

National Historic Trail
One national historic trail passes through Arkansas. The *Trail of Tears National Historic Trail* follows the route taken by the Cherokee as they were forced to move westward through nine states.

National Forests
Three national forests in Arkansas cover approximately 2.9 million acres (1.2 million ha). The largest is *Ouachita National Forest*, which continues into Oklahoma.

State Parks and Forests
Arkansas's state park system features and maintains more than 50 state parks and recreation areas, including *Crater of Diamonds State Park*, which contains the only diamond-producing site in the world that is open to the public. *Devil's Den State Park*, *Mammoth Spring State Park*, and *Historic Washington State Park* are other popular state parks.

SPORTS TEAMS

★ ★ ★

NCAA Teams (Division I)

Arkansas State University *Red Wolves*
University of Arkansas–Fayetteville *Razorbacks*
University of Arkansas–Little Rock *Trojans*
University of Arkansas–Pine Bluff *Lions*

The Arkansas State women's basketball team takes on Oklahoma in 2007.

CULTURAL INSTITUTIONS

★ ★ ★

Libraries

The *University of Arkansas–Fayetteville* has the state's largest book collection.

The *Central Arkansas Library System* provides library services for Little Rock and the surrounding area.

Museums

The *University of Arkansas Museum* (Fayetteville) contains both historical and archaeological exhibits and artifacts.

The *Museum of Discovery* (Little Rock) features exhibits such as the masks of many cultures.

The *Delta Cultural Center* (Helena) offers exhibits in a restored 1912 train depot on the culture and heritage of the Arkansas Delta.

The *Hampson Museum* (Wilson) exhibits a collection of artifacts from the Mound Builder period.

The *Old State House Museum* (Little Rock) is dedicated to the history of Arkansas.

Performing Arts

The *Arkansas Symphony Orchestra* (Little Rock) performs pops and classical music, and features a youth orchestra program that offers student musicians the opportunity to perform onstage.

Ballet Arkansas (Little Rock) provides world-class dance performances of classical and modern works.

Universities and Colleges

In 2011, Arkansas had 11 public and 16 private institutions of higher learning.

★ ANNUAL EVENTS

January–March

The Gallery Walk in Hot Springs (first Friday of every month)

Jonquil Festival in Old Washington State Park (March)

April–June

Arkansas Folk Festival and Arkansas Craft Guild Spring Show in Mountain View (April)

Springfest in Fayetteville (April)

Toad Suck Daze in Conway (May)

Quapaw Quarter Spring Tour of Historic Homes in Little Rock (May)

Riverfest in Little Rock (May)

Old Fort Days Rodeo in Fort Smith (May)

Pink Tomato Festival in Warren (June)

Riverfront Bluesfest in Fort Smith (June)

July–September

Peach Festival in Clarksville (July)

Rodeo of the Ozarks in Springdale (July)

Fayetteville Roots Festival in Fayetteville (August)

White River Water Carnival in Batesville (August or September)

Hope Watermelon Festival (August)

Arkansas State Fiddlers' Championship in Mountain View (September)

Antique Car Festival in Eureka Springs (September)

Four States Fair and Rodeo in Texarkana (September)

Bikes, Blues & BBQ Rally in Fayetteville (September)

Arkansas State Fair in Little Rock (late September/early October)

October–December

King Biscuit Blues Festival in Helena (October)

National Wild Turkey Calling Contest and Turkey Trot Festival in Yellville (October)

Herb Harvest Festival in Mountain View (October)

Arkansas Rice Festival in Weiner (October)

Original Ozark Folk Festival in Eureka Springs (October)

World's Championship Duck Calling Contest in Stuttgart (November)

BIOGRAPHICAL DICTIONARY

John Hanks Alexander (1864–1894), born in Helena, was the first African American officer in the U.S. armed forces to hold a command position. A graduate of the U.S. Military Academy, he later taught military tactics at Wilberforce University in Ohio.

Gilbert Maxwell Anderson (1880–1971) was a film actor who starred in the first Western, *The Great Train Robbery* (1903). Born in Little Rock and raised in Pine Bluff, he portrayed the character Broncho Billy in more than 400 movies.

Mabel Washbourne Anderson (1863–1949) wrote articles and books about Cherokee history and way of life.

Maya Angelou See page 81.

Harry Ashmore (1916–1998) won the Pulitzer Prize for a series of *Arkansas Gazette* editorials covering the desegregation crisis at Little Rock Central High School. He also wrote several books, including *Arkansas. A Bicentennial History* (1978).

Daisy Bates See page 66.

Gretha Boston (1959–) is an opera singer and stage actress who won a Tony Award in 1995 for portraying Queenie in the Broadway musical *Showboat*. Born and raised in Crossett, she was the first Arkansan to win the prestigious acting award.

Lou Brock (1939–), a native of El Dorado, was inducted into the Baseball Hall of Fame in 1985. In 1977, he broke baseball's base-stealing record, and since 1991 has remained ranked second in career steals.

Big Bill Broonzy (1893–1958) was one of America's most influential blues musicians. Born in Jefferson County, his most popular songs include "Midnight Special," "Key to the Highway," and "C. C. Rider."

Dee Brown (1908–2002) was an award-winning author and historian. He wrote books such as *Bury My Heart at Wounded Knee*, which tells the history of the settling of the western United States from the perspective of Native Americans, and *America Spa*, a history of Hot Springs. He was raised in Stephens.

Paul "Bear" Bryant

Paul "Bear" Bryant (1913–1983) was a college football coach whose teams at the University of Alabama won six college football championships. Born in Moro Bottom and raised in Fordyce, he picked up his nickname when he wrestled a bear at Fordyce Theater.

Lou Brock

Chester Burnett (1910–1976), better known as Howlin' Wolf, was one of the greatest blues singers ever. His influential songs include "Smokestack Lightning" and "Spoonful." His family moved to Wilson in 1933.

Sarah Caldwell (1924–2006) was a music conductor who was raised in Fayetteville. She later founded the Opera Company of Boston and was the first woman to conduct at New York's Metropolitan Opera.

Glen Campbell (1936–) is a country singer whose hits include "Rhinestone Cowboy" and "Gentle on My Mind." He was born and raised in Delight.

Hattie Wyatt Caraway See page 59.

Johnny Cash (1932–2003) was an influential American singer and songwriter. In a career that spanned nearly 50 years, he sold more than 90 million records. His hit songs included "Ring of Fire," "Folsom Prison Blues," and "I Walk the Line." He was born in Kingsland.

Wesley Clark (1944–) was a four-star general in the U.S. Army and the commander of the Supreme Headquarters Allied Powers Europe. He grew up in Little Rock.

Johnny Cash

Eldridge Cleaver

Powell Clayton See page 50.

Eldridge Cleaver (1935–1998) was an African American political activist in the 1960s. The Wabbaseka native was a leader of the Black Panther Party. He wrote several autobiographies, including *Soul on Ice* and *Soul on Fire*.

Bill Clinton See page 95.

Milton Crenchaw See page 75.

John Daly (1966–) is a successful professional golfer. He played golf at Dardanelle High School and the University of Arkansas.

Jay "Dizzy" Dean (1910–1974) was a Baseball Hall of Fame pitcher who won 150 games during his career. The Lucas native became a hero for many poor young Arkansans during the Depression.

Bill Dickey (1907–1993) was a baseball catcher for the New York Yankees for 17 seasons, playing on championship teams alongside stars Babe Ruth and Lou Gehrig. Raised in Arkansas, he attended Little Rock College. Dickey was inducted into the Baseball Hall of Fame in 1954.

William Dillard See page 106.

David Owen Dodd See page 49.

Jimmy Driftwood (1907–1998) was a folksinger and songwriter from Mountain View. He wrote hits such as "The Battle of New Orleans" and was involved in the creation of the Ozark Folk Center.

Ronnie Dunn (1953–) is part of the country music duo Brooks & Dunn. The El Dorado native is a member of the Arkansas Entertainers Hall of Fame.

Orval Faubus (1910–1994) was a controversial six-time governor who rose to national prominence by forcefully opposing the integration of Little Rock Central High School.

J. William Fulbright (1905–1995) served in the U.S. Congress for 32 years. He grew up in Fayetteville, graduated from the University of Arkansas, and returned to teach at the university's law school in 1936. The Fulbright Program, a U.S. State Department program that awards scholarships to college students and academic scholars to study or teach abroad, is named for him.

Ellen Gilchrist (1935–) is a noted author and a writing professor at the University of Arkansas. She won the National Book Award for her short-story collection *Victory Over Japan* (1984).

Ellen Gilchrist

Ernest Green (1941–) was the first African American to graduate from Little Rock Central High School. He went on to earn a bachelor's and a master's degree from Michigan State University.

John Grisham (1955–) is a best-selling author who has written legal thrillers such as *The Firm*, *A Time to Kill*, and *The Pelican Brief*. He was born in Jonesboro.

Levon Helm (1940–2012) was the drummer and vocalist for the rock group the Band. He also acted in films such as *Coal Miner's Daughter* and *The Right Stuff*. He grew up on his family's cotton farm in Marvell.

Barbara Hendricks (1948–) is an opera singer, born in Stephens, who has performed in opera houses worldwide. She is also a human rights activist.

Mike Huckabee (1955–), born in Hope, was the governor of Arkansas from 1996 to 2007. In 2008, he launched an unsuccessful campaign for the Republican presidential nomination.

Barbara Hendricks

Johnnie Bryan Hunt (1927–2006) was an Arkansas businessperson who founded the nation's largest trucking company. Born near Heber Springs, he started J. B. Hunt Transport Services in Lowell in 1969.

136

John H. Johnson

John H. Johnson (1918–2005) was the founder and publisher of *Ebony*, *Jet*, and other magazines aimed at African American readers. Born in Arkansas City, he moved to Chicago with his family at age 14 and later studied at the University of Chicago. He started his first magazine in 1942.

Jerry Jones (1942–) is the owner of the NFL's Dallas Cowboys. The North Little Rock native played on the 1964 University of Arkansas team that won the national college football championship and then became a successful businessperson in the oil industry.

Scott Joplin (1868–1917) was a composer best known for ragtime songs such as "Maple Leaf Rag." Ragtime is a type of piano-driven dance music that was popular in the early 1900s. He grew up in Texarkana.

Louis Jordan (1908–1975) was a saxophonist, singer, and bandleader who greatly influenced jazz and rock 'n' roll. Born in Brinkley, he joined his father's traveling band at age 15. His hits included "Ain't Nobody Here But Us Chickens."

Alan Ladd (1913–1964) was a popular movie actor during the 1940s and 1950s. Born in Hot Springs, he is best known for his performances in *Shane*, *Two Years Before the Mast*, and *The Glass Key*.

Charles "Sonny" Liston (c. 1930–1970) was the world heavyweight boxing champion from 1962 to 1964. He was born in St. Francis County in eastern Arkansas.

Douglas MacArthur (1880–1964) was a five-star general during World War II. The Little Rock native was commander of Allied forces in the Pacific and accepted the Japanese surrender in 1945.

Mark Martin (1959–) is a successful race-car driver on the NASCAR circuit. Born and raised in Batesville, he raced on dirt tracks in Arkansas before his NASCAR career.

Patsy Montana (1908–1996) was known as the Queen of Country Western Music. Born Ruby Blevins in Hope, she had the first hit record by a female country singer, "I Want to Be a Cowboy's Sweetheart."

Scottie Pippen (1965–) won six NBA championships while playing for the Chicago Bulls. Born and raised in Hamburg, he played at the University of Central Arkansas in Conway before playing in the NBA.

Scottie Pippen

Brooks Robinson (1937–), born in Little Rock, was a professional baseball player who played his entire 23-year career for the Baltimore Orioles. Robinson was inducted into the Baseball Hall of Fame in 1983.

Winthrop Rockefeller See page 102.

Pharoah Sanders (1940–) is a jazz saxophonist known for his experimental style. Born and raised in Little Rock, he has played with jazz legends Sun Ra and John Coltrane and has had a successful solo career.

Lottie Shackelford See page 92.

Margarita Solórzano See page 77.

Mary Steenburgen (1953–) is an Academy Award–winning actress who has appeared in films such as *Ragtime* and *Parenthood*. She was born in Newport.

William Grant Still (1895–1978) is one of America's greatest composers. Raised in Little Rock, he began composing symphonies and popular music in 1924. His *Afro-American Symphony* (1930) is his best-known work.

Edward Durell Stone (1902–1978) was a leading figure in the development of modern architecture in the United States. His most famous designs include Radio City Music Hall in New York City, the John F. Kennedy Center for the Performing Arts in Washington, D.C., and the Standard Oil Building in Chicago. He was born in Fayetteville.

Pharoah Sanders

Louise Thaden (1905–1979) was an airplane pilot who set numerous flying records and won many major events in the 1920s and 1930s. She was born in Bentonville.

Billy Bob Thornton (1955–) is an award-winning director, screenwriter, and actor who has appeared in films such as *Friday Night Lights*. He is from Malvern.

Henri de Tonti See page 37.

Conway Twitty (1933–1993) had more number-one country records than any other musician. His hits include "Linda on My Mind" and "Louisiana Woman, Mississippi Man" (a duet with Loretta Lynn). Born Harold Jenkins and raised in Helena, he took his stage name from Conway, Arkansas, and Twitty, Texas.

Don Tyson (1930–2011) took over his family's food business in 1967 and transformed it into the nation's largest poultry and beef processing company.

Cephas Washburn (1793–1860) was a Christian missionary who worked with the Cherokee people of northwest Arkansas.

Sonny Boy Williamson (c. 1912–1965) See page 83.

Mary Steenburgen

RESOURCES

★ ★ ★

BOOKS

Nonfiction

Aretha, David. *The Story of the Little Rock Nine and School Desegregation in Photographs.* Berkeley Heights, N.J.: Enslow Publishers, 2014.

Benoit, Peter. *The Louisiana Purchase.* New York: Children's Press, 2012.

Domnauer, Teresa. *The Lewis & Clark Expedition.* New York: Children's Press, 2013.

Hopper, Shay E., T. Harri Baker, and Jane Browning. *An Arkansas History for Young People.* Fayetteville, Ark.: University of Arkansas Press, 2008.

Kissock, Heather. *Caddo: American Indian Art and Culture.* New York: Weigl Publishers, 2011.

Roberts, Russell. *Scott Joplin.* Hockessin, Del.: Mitchell Lane Publishers, 2013.

Teske, Steven. *Natural State Notables: 21 Famous People from Arkansas.* Little Rock, Ark.: Butler Central Books, 2013.

Young, Jeff C. *Hernando de Soto: Spanish Conquistador in the Americas.* Berkeley Heights, N.J.: Enslow Publishers, 2009.

Fiction

Branscum, Robbie. *The Murder of Hound Dog Bates.* New York: Penguin, 1995.

Crofford, Emily. *A Place to Belong.* Minneapolis: Lerner, 1993.

Greene, Bette. *I've Already Forgotten Your Name, Philip Hall!* New York: HarperCollins, 2002.

Greene, Bette. *Summer of My German Soldier.* New York: Penguin, 2006.

Grisham, John. *A Painted House.* New York: Doubleday, 2001.

Massey, Ellen Gray. *Mysteries of the Ozarks.* Branson, Mo.: Skyward, 2004.

Portis, Charles. *True Grit.* New York: Penguin, 2007.

Strauss, Victoria. *Guardian of the Hills.* New York: HarperCollins, 1995.

Traylor, Betty. *Buckaroo.* New York: Random House, 1999.

FACTS FOR NOW

Visit this Scholastic Web site for more information on Arkansas:
www.factsfornow.scholastic.com
Enter the keyword **Arkansas**

INDEX

★ ★ ★

AUTHOR'S TIPS AND SOURCE NOTES

★ ★ ★

To research this book, I began at the library. Harry Ashmore's *Arkansas: A Bicentennial History* was a great resource, providing in-depth information on Arkansas's history from statehood until the late 1970s. I also used C. Fred Williams's *A Documentary History of Arkansas* and Ben Johnson's *Arkansas in Modern America*. The Internet also provided much useful information. I used search engines such as Google to find Web sites to answer specific questions, such as how many pounds of rice are grown in Arkansas each year and what books Maya Angelou wrote.